# Onward

## A Life on a Sailboat

### By Mark Tedesco

Academia Publications
Copyright © 2024 by Mark Tedesco

Onward: A Life on a Sailboat - Mark Tedesco

Cover Designer: Karen Snave
I. Edition: September 2024
Library of Congress Cataloging-in-Publication Data
Mark Tedesco

ISBN: 9798330297955 (paperback)
ISBN: 9798330297962 (ebook)

1. Travel writing 2. Fiction 3. Memoir 4. Travel tips

© Academia Publications
Marktedesco.com

# Table of Contents

# Chapter 1
# Out of the Depths

A life that springs from death sounds like a cliche, but that is how my story begins.

I was in my second year as a business major at UC Santa Cruz, asleep in my dorm, when I heard it. It started as knocking, which then became banging. I looked at the clock: three in the morning. "Jovanny. Is your name Jovanny?" the officer asked, shining a flashlight in my face as I opened the door. "Yeah, that's me," I said. "Can I come in, son?" I didn't want to invite him in, so I asked, "What's this about?" He put his flashlight down, looked into my eyes, and said, "It's your folks. Please, can I come in?" I moved aside, turned on the light, and let him enter. When I turned, he asked if I wanted to sit. "No; what happened?" "I don't know how to say this, Jovanny. Your folks were hit by a drunk driver earlier this evening on Highway 1. We did everything we could, but we couldn't save them. We airlifted them to the hospital, where they were pronounced dead. We had a hell of a time trying to find you. Why don't you get dressed and come to the hospital with me."

# A Life on a Sailboat

The rest of that night was a blur; I remember putting some clothes on, getting into the police car, and walking into a hospital. As I was led into a room to identify the bodies, I remember thinking that it must be a big mixup; mom and dad had probably stopped to eat and were out of cell phone range. There is no way that they could be dead!

When they did pull back the sheet, it was my mom. And then my dad. The first part of my life was over at that moment.

I have fond memories of my parents. They had a good balance: My dad was practical, while my mom was a dreamer. My dad and I shared a love for water, and he made a career out of his passion for watersports and boating.

He built up a successful business, starting from the lowest job at the marina in San Diego. He went from cleaning boats to repairing engines to selling yachts. He was a man who dared to carve a life around his passion.

I remember my mom as more of an adventurer. She loved planning vacations to other countries and exploring new areas. By the time I turned fifteen, we had sailed the Mediterranean, biked through the Alps, hiked the Andes in Venezuela, and water skied off the coast of Rhodes.

Throughout my childhood and young adulthood, my parents instilled in me three key values that have remained. Firstly, they encouraged me to find my own path in life, to follow my passions

and interests. Secondly, they taught me the importance of seeking happiness and pursuing a meaningful life. Lastly, they emphasized the significance of building solid relationships and cherishing the people I care about. These lessons have had a profound impact on me.

I was finishing my senior year in high school when I applied to UC Santa Cruz and I think we were all surprised when I was accepted. "Congratulations, son!" my father exclaimed when I received my acceptance letter. "What are you looking forward to at UC?" my mother asked. I replied, "Surfing between classes." My parents looked at each other with concern but didn't say anything. To ease their worries, I added, "I'm also looking forward to my studies!"

Perhaps surfing was not a great reason to choose a university, but I was barely eighteen, and being out on the water was everything to me.

I can't say that I excelled in my classes during those first years, but I did keep afloat, got passing grades and made time for surfing with friends.

Then everything changed.

I walked in a daze from class to class after their deaths, pretending to be okay. College friends noticed a change and later told me I seemed withdrawn. I kept my studies up, but my heart wasn't in it.

I had never really thought about my future. I had assumed that I would get a business degree and join my dad in his business after college. However, the idea of taking over my dad's business without him didn't feel like the right path. In fact, it felt empty and depressing. As I completed my semester and tried to figure out my future, my dad's business manager kindly agreed to keep the business open and running.

I made it a point to surf every day to clear my thoughts and ease my worries. During those early morning surfs, I contemplated my life and the direction I wanted to take. I found myself asking deeper questions, especially about what makes me happy.

While riding the waves one morning, I asked myself, "What was the happiest moment in my life?" Looking back, I realized the happiest time of my life was when I sailed across the Mediterranean with my folks.

In the following days and weeks, I couldn't help but daydream about sailing across the sea again. It almost felt as if the Mediterranean was calling out to me.

Jim was my college friend and fellow surfer who stood by me during those difficult times. One morning, after our early morning surf, I confided in him.

# Onward

"Why not?" he asked. "Huh?" was my reply. "Why the fuck not?" I looked at him, wondering what he was talking about. "Why not create a new life for yourself on a sailboat? Why not take that dream, shove it into reality, and make it happen? Why the fuck not?" he said empathically.

I remember laughing because it sounded so ridiculous. But unbeknownst to Jim, he had planted a seed.

Over the following weeks, I wondered if living on a sailboat was a crazy idea. Yes, it seemed ridiculous because I couldn't see how. How would I fund it? Where would I live when it was not sailing weather? What about safety? Where would I sail to? How would I learn enough about sailing and routes to avoid dying at sea?

But the questions didn't stop my imagination from considering the idea. In fact, a few months later, I told Jim: "Call me crazy, but I'm going to see what it takes to live on a sailboat." "Crazy? No! I call that 'balls,' my friend," was his reply.

But if I went away on a sailing adventure, I had no idea what to do with my dad's business.

I met with my dad's business manager to discuss selling it. He informed me that the business was worth millions, but unfortunately, he didn't have the money to buy it himself. He did offer to help me find investors, though. I also discovered that my dad had set up a trust fund for me, which, while not a lot, would provide me with some monthly income.

A few weeks later, with the help of a financial advisor recommended by the business manager, I learned that I could sell the business and invest the proceeds in setting up a fund that would cover my expenses for my future as long as I kept my yearly expenses within a specific limit.

After comparing my budget to the projected cost of a small house near a marina on the Adriatic, which included the boat and maintenance, docking fees, and monthly expenses, I realized that if I stayed within my budget, the investments resulting from the sale of the business, along with the trust, would enable me to live on a sailboat without needing to have a job.

"Well? Will you fucking do this, or let life pass you by?" Jim asked when I shared the results of my fact-finding.

I had decided by then and replied confidently, "I'm going to do this, Jim." He jumped up and yelled, "Fucking A!" Then I stopped him and added, "But if it doesn't work out, can I crash with you until I get my life together again?" "Any fucking time!" he said.

Things started moving quickly; I transferred to UC Santa Barbara, where I changed my major to geography and completed it in four semesters. Next, I set my sights on finding a home base in Brindisi, Italy, locating a suitable boat, and taking sailing lessons. When my dad's business sold, I hired a financial manager to help me create a steady income stream that would last me for as long as needed.

## Onward

The ball was moving, the train had left the station, and I looked forward to my new life.

Two years after I received that awful news about my parents, I left friends and relatives behind as my life in California faded into history, and my life on a sailboat began.

I never looked back.

# Chapter 2
# Amalfi and Friendship

The years in California faded as my adventure on the sea became my life. Over a decade later, I am living my dream on a sailboat, with a home in Brindisi when I'm not at sea.

When I first started sailing, I wanted to avoid the Amalfi coast because I thought it was too touristy. However, after becoming close friends with Antonio and Giovanna, who are like family to me, I have returned to the area many times.

In my experience, there are three distinct categories of sailors besides those in the Navy. The first group consists of wealthy individuals with a yacht and crew. The second group includes independent sailors like myself, who find ways to finance their sailing adventures. The third group is made up of working-class sailors who have turned their passion for sailing into a career. Antonio belongs to the third category, as he is a true sailor. He always dreamed of sailing, and we had some fantastic adventures together.

However, the realities of life hit him hard when he got married and had his first child. He settled down in Salerno and started his own tourist sailing business. Since then, he and Giovanna have had two more children, making it a total of three: two girls and a boy named Tony Jr. I am Tony's godfather.

I was at my base in Brindisi when Giovanna called one morning. "Gio, come stai?" After some small talk, I asked her, "How is Antonio, and what's going on?" Giovanna sighed. "He is driving me crazy these past weeks because he feels so imprisoned here. Gio, you know Antonio as well as anyone, perhaps even better. He wants to be free; he wants a life like yours. Sometimes, I feel like the kids and I are tying him down. I can see it in his eyes…" I interrupted her. "No, non è così…." But then she broke in. "Gio, you don't have to try to console me; we know each other well. Antonio is an adventurer, and I don't begrudge him that. But, every once in a while, he needs to be free; he needs to experience the water, the wind, and the carelessness of life. I understand that. So I am calling you to ask you, as his friend, to take Antonio off my hands, to take him sailing for a week, ten days, or even more! When the weather clears, please plan that trip! He can get this longing out of his system for a while; you know how that works!"

I did know how that works.

Several times, Antonio had stayed with me in Brindisi during the off-season, and we had taken some day sailing trips when the weather permitted. He always had the same pattern: he arrived at my place pensive and worried about family and business. After a few days on the water, he loosened up and became fun to be with again.

Antonio and I got along well, so agreeing to Giovanna's proposal was easy.

"But there are a few things to remember," she continued. "Under no circumstances are you to tell Antonio about this call. If he finds out, he will never go. But he needs to go. If he keeps this longing suppressed for much longer, he will resent me and the children. He is already short-tempered, and I know exactly why. He hasn't gone sailing for himself in two years; the last time was with you."

I agreed but asked, "What do you have in mind?" Giovanna paused. "I haven't thought of the particulars. You can come here in your boat and pick him up next month. If you do that, there is less chance of him backing out. You could propose this to him. He will object and say that he has to earn money for the family, has responsibilities, and can't get free when there is good sailing weather. You need to say, 'Speak with Giovanna.' That's all. I know him; he will bring the matter to me, and I will make sure he goes. Gio, can I count on you?"

I laughed and said, "Certo/certainly." Then I continued, "But what about you during that time? You would be alone with three kids for weeks! Is that what you want?" This time, Giovanna laughed. "I already have that figured out. My mother, my brother, his family, and I will rent a villa together in Sicily. We already have it reserved. The next step is to convince Antonio."

Antonio must be getting seriously on her nerves since Giovanna wanted to nail this down. "I will call him tonight." After many thank yous, she hung up.

I understood Antonio's craving. I felt it when I was in Brindisi for too long, like a desire that gets inside you, so small that you barely notice. Then, it starts to grow, gently nudging the feelings, causing a slight sense of dissatisfaction with the routine of life. It manifests in impatience with others. It then surfaces in comments and reactions that reveal resentment towards the weather, circumstances, or people.

I get it; I've been there, and apparently, Antonio was already there.

"I can't. Giovanna would kill me," he responded when I called him later. "No, she won't. Talk to her before you decide," I insisted. But he was adamant. "Plus, Gio, I have a family to support. I would love to go with you for a few weeks, but who will pay the bills? In a month, the tourist season begins. You know I can't take days off during that time. Sure, I'd love to go, but I can't. I am sorry."

I looked at the phone; this will be more difficult than I thought. I needed time to think, so I invented an excuse to get off the phone. "I will call you tomorrow, my friend. I have something to do on the boat before I lose the light. A domani," I said and hung up.

When Antonio called me the next day, his opening words were, "Gio, maybe I was too quick to say 'no' to your proposal yesterday. Let me think about it. After all, life is short." As he spoke, I imagined him going to Giovanna after our phone call and saying, "You won't believe the crazy idea that Gio just shared with me...." Then I imagined her replying, "What's so crazy about that?" They probably went back and forth all evening until Antonio stopped worrying about responsibilities and started thinking about happiness. "So Gio, I am not saying yes yet; you know I'd love to do that, but should I?" I laughed and said, "I've done many things that I shouldn't have done and ended up being all the more happy because of them." Antonio, of course, objected, "But I am married, I have a family; I can't just run off..." I interrupted him. "If your concern is your family, what does Giovanna say?" He was struck silent, so I prodded him. "What does she say about this, Antonio? She doesn't want you to go?" "I need to speak with her again," was all he replied.

A few days later, I got a three-word text from Giovanna. "Mission accomplished. Thanks."

About five weeks later, I left Brindisi and sailed towards Salerno; I would pick Antonio up, Giovanna and the kids would go to Sicily, and everyone agreed to leave their cares at home.

When I arrived at Antonio's place, he wasn't ready yet. He seemed lost in thought, still uncertain whether he was making the right decision. He hadn't even started packing his bag and was pacing back and forth. "My friend, the family is fine. It's time to take care of yourself. You'll be a better man because of it. Don't worry, let me help you pack your things," I reassured him.

We finally left his house and headed towards the marina. Before getting on board, he called Giovanna, asking if she and the kids were OK. They were fine, having left just a few hours ago. I wished he would relax, so I came up with an idea before pushing off.

We threw his suitcase onto the boat, and then I took him to a nearby cafe for a morning spritz. "Here's to life, adventure, and happiness!" I toasted as we clinked our glasses. After that, we returned to the boat and got ready to set sail. When Antonio complained again about not wanting to leave, I reminded him of our toast to adventure. I knew he would feel better once we were out on the water.

From that moment on, whenever one brought up a concern or worry, the other would say, "The toast, my friend," or just "toast." It became our mantra.

Antonio was tired of planning routes and organizing trips, so I took the responsibility. We had a ten-day itinerary, but I secretly planned to extend it to two weeks. I decided to leave the Amalfi area so that Antonio wouldn't be reminded of work and would become a more pleasant companion. Therefore, we headed north towards the Italian Riviera from where we would continue our journey to the south of France.

I had planned a memorable journey from Salerno to Liguria, which would take more than a day. We'd be sleeping at sea, which was perfect as we'd been on land too long. To start our adventure, I used my connections to book a berth at the marina in Portofino for the following day, despite it being an expensive area. The beauty of the place made it worth the cost.

Antonio had no idea about my plan. With a gentle breeze, we used the sails and kept the motor off. Antonio seemed quiet on the first day, and I wasn't sure if he was enjoying himself or preoccupied with work and family. I decided to give him some space and let him be, knowing that this was just the start of our adventure.

As the sun set, we rolled up the sails and gently glided while I started preparing dinner. I moved the grill onto the deck, and the aroma of grilled steaks soon filled the air. I opened a bottle of excellent Tuscan white wine, Vernaccia di San Gimignano, as the steaks sizzled and the vegetables grilled to perfection. The sun had disappeared below the horizon, and the entire sky turned a beautiful shade of orange. "To life," I said as we clinked glasses. "Gio, are you sure about having white wine with beef?" Antonio asked as he emptied his glass. "Yes, for now, but with dinner, I have a bottle of Brunello given to me by a dear lady..." Antonio laughed. "So many 'dear ladies,' Gio!" We clinked glasses again, toasted, and emptied our glasses. I left Antonio to tend to the steaks and called out, "Have another glass for me!" He did.

The first stars appeared as we cut into our rare steaks, tasted the grilled marinated mushrooms with asparagus, and gorged ourselves on sliced tomatoes with olives and cucumbers, followed by a fruit salad and chocolate cake. "Gio, you have done it again; the perfect meal on a perfect evening," Antonio said as he raised his glass of Brunello.

I can't remember when I dozed off or how I got to my bunk below. Maybe it was the great food, the too many glasses of wine, or the peace I felt.

I woke up around three in the morning and looked over at Antonio's bunk. I called out "Anto!" but he didn't answer. I sat up and realized he wasn't there.

I climbed up on deck and found him sitting in the deck chair, wide awake, looking out over the water. I sat next to him. The Antonio I had known had returned. "What are you thinking about, my friend?" I asked. Without turning, he said, "How great life is and how lucky I am." I then rose, patted his shoulder, and went back to bed.

To make the most of our trip to Portofino, I planned our journey so that we would reach our destination early in the morning. It was still before 6 o'clock when I called out to Antonio, "Buon giorno! We're almost there!" He was still asleep, so I prodded him, "You'll lose the day if you keep sleeping!" He replied in a groggy voice, "Where are we? Is there coffee? What time is it?" I told him, "There's coffee on the stove; come up and see for yourself where we are!"

The morning view of Portofino from the water is indescribable. One should never see this town for the first time from the land. Once Antonio climbed up to the deck, blinked his eyes, and looked at the view, he said, "It is so beautiful that I want to cry."

We docked the boat in the berth I had reserved and headed towards a cafe with a stunning view but with overpriced coffee. "This is too expensive!" Antonio protested. "My friend," I replied, "Ten euros for a coffee in Portofino, with this view, is worth every penny. Let's enjoy the moment; it's just a coffee," I said as we walked in. The staff appeared unfriendly and snobbish as they looked us up and down. However, I didn't let their attitude discourage us. I signaled Antonio to follow me, and we picked our own table with the best view. We then asked the waiter near the door to bring us two coffees and the bill. He seemed annoyed but complied with our request and didn't bother us afterward.

Since neither Antonio nor I wanted to sit in a cafe all day, we decided to take the three-hour hike from Portofino to Camogli. From there we could experience the views while avoiding most tourists. "I'm not walking six hours today, so there better be a bus back!" Antonio said as we set out. "You sound like an old man," I replied, jokingly. We went back and forth in this manner for the first half hour. Then, the view opened up when we reached the top of the ridge, and we were struck silent.

Antonio whispered in a hushed tone, as if we were in a church, "If I could see this view every day,

Onward

I would die content." I chuckled and asked, "Do you want me to help?" as I playfully nudged him toward the cliff. "Gio!" he exclaimed, grabbing my arm to steady himself.

Ancient olive trees and maritime pines surrounded us as we continued to follow the path. The route would occasionally open up to reveal stunning bay views before leading us back among the trees. We stopped at one of these openings to rest, drink water, and have snacks I had packed. While munching on some cheese and gazing at the sea, Antonio wondered aloud, "Do the people who live here and see this every day appreciate it? Or do they become like those snobby waiters who take it for granted?" I laughed, and Antonio continued, "I already don't like the residents of Portofino, even though I haven't met any!" We toasted our bottled waters and laughed.

We heard a woman's voice coming from a short distance away as we stood there. She said, "I live here." We looked at each other and then turned towards the voice coming from behind a shrub. I peered around the plant and saw a woman in her forties with long black hair, dark eyes, and a beautiful figure. She was taking a drag from her cigarette as she gazed at the water. Antonio stumbled over his words, trying to apologize. "I'm so sorry. We didn't mean to..." She waved his words away. "It's fine. I can't stand those waiters, either. You probably went to..." Here, she mentioned the name of the cafe

17

where we had gotten our coffee. "I never go there. I would never go there. Just because you work at a cafe with a nice view, you think you're better than everyone else? Give me a break," she said, taking another drag. Then she laughed.

"I'm Emma, by the way. Who are you, and why are you here? Sorry if I am direct," she asked as she turned towards us.

"My name is Jovanny, but my friends call me Gio. This is Antonio. We're here for adventure," I replied. Glancing at Antonio, I added, "And friendship."

Emma then looked both of us up and down and asked, "Are you a couple?"

I laughed and said, "That's why I can't get a date! Antonio, stop looking at me that way!" I joked. He shoved my shoulder towards the edge, then grabbed my arm. "OK, dear," he said.

I pushed him back and bowed to Emma.

We sat next to her at her invitation, with the sea below and the olive groves behind us. After a few minutes, Emma asked, "Why did you come here?" Antonio replied, "It's the routine that can weigh you down. I have a wonderful life with a beautiful wife and great kids. But I get so lost in all the obligations, worries, appointments, expenses, and long-term planning that I forget the important things."

Emma interrupted, "But what is important?" Without any hesitation, Antonio replied, "Happiness."

Emma took one last drag of her cigarette, which was on the verge of burning out, and carefully placed it in her portable ashtray.

"Are you happy, Emma, living in this place and having this view every day?" Antonio asked a personal question, but Emma didn't seem to mind.

"Would looking at this every day be enough to make you happy?" she asked both of us.

Antonio nodded, but her question made me pause, and I replied, "Almost."

Emma agreed.

"That 'almost' is the key. That 'almost' is like the tiny fly in a huge pot of the best honey. Even though the flavor is the same with or without the fly, that tiny creature, that tiny 'almost,' can change everything."

She asked me, "What is that 'almost' for you, Jovanny?"

Though we had just introduced ourselves, we were talking like old friends.

I glanced at Antonio, who was waiting for my answer.

"Sometimes, I want more of what Antonio has." I surprised myself when I admitted this in front of my friend. He was smiling and said, "What? You're kidding, right?"

I kept looking at him until he realized it was not a joke.

"That's funny because sometimes I dream of having Gio's life. It's like I want both: I want my life, and I want Gio's life. Is that the way it is for you?" he asked. I nodded. "That's my 'almost,'" I replied.

I hoped she wouldn't take out another cigarette, but she did: lit it up, took a drag, and looked out over the sea.

"What is your 'almost,' Emma?" I asked. She smiled and turned towards us. "Why don't you two come for dinner tonight? Our place is just over that ridge, overlooking the harbor."

We told her we didn't have the right clothes, but she dismissed it. We claimed to have dinner plans, but she asked where. We even lied, saying we were leaving that evening, but she asked us when.

"We don't bite. It's my husband and a few friends. We're just going to grill some fish and vegetables and eat outside. Very informal. Not a party."

"But why invite us?" Antonio asked in a tone that suggested we were unworthy of such an invitation. Emma found his response amusing and responded, "Why not? You're interesting, involved with life, and on an adventure of friendship." She continued, "But if you're not interested, that's fine. It was just a thought..." I interjected, "We'll be there. Just let us know when and where."

After leaving Emma on the cliff, we continued our hike until we both became sweaty and tired. I jokingly asked Antonio if it was too much for him: "Of course not, I'm a strong man!" he said, panting. I then noticed a path leading to a small beach below and suggested we go down there to relax in the water before heading back to the marina. Antonio didn't respond to my suggestion but instead rushed down towards the water, leaving me behind on the path.

When we got to the water, I jumped in naked, but Antonio kept his undies on; either way, nobody was around, so it wasn't a big deal. It felt cold when I plunged into the water, but it soon became the perfect temperature. I was in my element and swam out a bit while Antonio relaxed closer to shore. When I swam back, I found him floating on his back. "Gio!" he called. I swam next to him. "Don't you ever relax? Hiking, swimming, sailing, running, chasing, hiking, then more swimming... RELAX, my friend. Do you know how to float?" he asked. "Of course," I said, as I made some feeble attempts but kept sinking.

"I CAN float, but just not right now," I said as I left him to swim out further again.

As I returned to the beach, I found Antonio sunbathing. I lay beside him, put my hat on my face, and closed my eyes. After half an hour, Antonio woke me up and said, "Gio! Are you awake?" I replied, "Yes," without uncovering my face. Antonio said, "I just wanted to say how amazing this is. Thank you for pulling me with you, my friend." I started to say, "Well, Giovanna..." but then stopped. I didn't want to give away our secret.

I thought briefly, uncovered my face, and replied, "Giovanna encouraged you also." Antonio nodded and then added, "She probably needed a break! I haven't been very nice lately. I get stressed and worried and imagine how life could be different, which isn't very nice to her. She is everything to me, Gio." "I know, Antonio. Giovanna is amazing."

It was time to get dressed and head back to the marina since we had an engagement that evening and could not show up smelling of seawater.

"Where's the bus?" Antonio asked when we got to the top of the ridge.

There was no bus.

The hike back seemed longer, even though it took us less time. We needed to return to my boat, rest, clean up, and then show up at Emma's dinner. But when we got to town, I suggested we stop before heading to the marina. "Antonio! Let's take fifteen minutes; you won't regret it." He followed me, probably too worn out to object. We sat at an outdoor table at a gelateria/ice cream shop near the center of Portofino. The prices were inflated, but the gelato was delicious, and the people-watching was amusing. "New rich!" Antonio whispered, nodding to a passerby in designer clothing. "Fake rich!" I whispered back, nodding toward an American couple. "Not rich!" Antonio responded, nodding toward me.

We used the marina showers to freshen up before crashing. Antonio texted his wife before dozing off; I sent my regards, set the alarm, and drifted off into my deepest two-hour nap in months.

"We finally found someone to marry Gio," I heard as Antonio's voice, chatting with Giovanna on his phone on the deck, roused me. "She's a millionaire, has a villa in Portofino, and invited us to dinner tonight...but there are two problems." Antonio paused, listening to Giovanna, and then continued, "First, she is married, so she has to get rid of her husband. Second, she thinks Gio is gay...." I laughed and shouted, "She thinks Antonio is gay too!" Giovanna must have said something because Antonio started laughing uncontrollably. He came down a few minutes later. "Giovanna sends her love. She also said you might have more chances with the husband. Hah!" I threw my pillow at him and rolled out of the bunk.

About an hour later, we walked up the private road to Emma's villa. We hadn't packed any formal clothes, so I was wearing blue jeans and a polo shirt, and Antonio was wearing jeans and one of my nicer T-shirts. "Are you nervous?" I asked him. He shrugged. "It's all part of the adventure. I will keep eating if I don't know what to say."

We approached the iron gates where a man was waiting. "Good evening. You are Signori Jovanny and Antonio, no?" Antonio looked at me and nodded. "Walk straight up that path until you see the pool on your right, beside the house. Go over to the pool area, and you will find the others," he said as he let us in.

Antonio was losing confidence and whispered, "What are we doing here, Gio? We can turn back and relax on the boat!" I stopped, looked at him, shook my head, and opened my mouth. Before I could speak, Antonio said, "I know what you will say: this is an adventure! Why miss an adventure?"

He laughed, then continued, "OK, Gio, let's do it. But if we make fools out of ourselves, I will never date you again!" We both laughed, continued up the path, spotted the pool, turned right, and stopped in our tracks. The infinity pool was on the edge of a rock formation that overlooked Portofino's bay; yachts bobbed in the harbor below, bathed in the setting sun's orange glow.

It was beautiful.

I stopped Antonio to take a photo of us, with the house/pool/sea/garden behind us. I sent it to our friend Matteo back in Brindisi with the phrase, "We are here now." Within seconds, I received a two-word response: "Vi odio" = I hate you.

Antonio then sent it to Giovanna, who responded, "Tell Gio to marry her." Emma was pretty, and, unfortunately, I must have said this to Antonio at some point because neither he nor Giovanna would leave it alone—the ups and downs of being single.

"Welcome-Benvenuti!" Emma called out as she approached, her dark hair shimmering in the setting sun. I was relieved to see her dressed informally in jeans.

She greeted us warmly and kissed us on both cheeks like old friends. "Are you taking photos for your wife and girlfriend?" she asked. Antonio didn't miss a beat and replied, "Wife, yes, but Gio doesn't have a girlfriend right now, a rare occurrence for him. So he will be looking for one tonight." I glared at him while he and Emma laughed. She locked her arms in ours and walked us to the other guests next to the pool. "Be good!" I mouthed to Antonio behind Emma's back.

Emma introduced us to her husband Paolo, who was grilling some fish with one hand and chatting on his cell phone with the other. He nodded and gave us a thumbs-up while discussing a business deal. He seemed older than Emma, slightly rotund, balding, sporting a red polo shirt with the collar turned up.

We also met Luca and Elena, friends visiting from Milan, Elia and Franco from Bologna, and finally, Stefano and Gabriella, locals. One thing that stood out to me about this group was that they dressed more formally than us, and their skin looked so flawless that it seemed like they had just come from a spa.

Emma kicked off her shoes and brought us two glasses of wine. Although she appeared relaxed, I felt awkward. We stood in a circle with the other guests, who seemed stiff and uncomfortable. Emma's husband was still on the phone discussing business. Emma broke the silence by saying, "I met two sailors today, so I brought them home with me." Everyone laughed, thinking it was a joke. She continued,

"Jovanny lives on a sailboat, always searching for adventure, and Antonio owns a boating business along the Amalfi coast." After a brief pause, the guests nodded politely. One of them, Elena, cleared her throat and asked, "How long have you lived on a boat?" I answered, "Since I was twenty-two." Elena replied, "Oh," politely disinterested.

"Would you like to see the sunset?" Emma asked. We went to the edge of their property, overlooking the harbor. "This is so beautiful," Antonio whispered as we looked out on the port; the waves looked like flames as they reflected the evening sun. "I envy anyone who could live in that beauty all the time! Just think how it would be to call a sailboat home!" I said jokingly. "Keep rubbing it in, Gio!" Antonio said.

As we gazed at the sunset, Emma said, "Have you ever noticed how difficult it is to describe beauty? Words can never fully capture its essence. All we can do is look at it." Just then, the first star appeared in the sky, and Antonio pointed it out. Emma then asked us, "What do you feel right now?" I replied, "Awe," while Antonio said, "Gratitude." Emma took a moment to answer, still looking at the sunset. "I feel peace, contentment, and joy," she said softly. Then, she added, "But I also feel sadness," glancing at her husband and friends.

"The fish!" Paolo cried out from the grill. "I was distracted and overcooked the fish," he said as he shook his head. Emma walked over and looked. "It's fine, dear. With all the other food we have, it will be perfect."

# Onward

Flaming torches illuminated the yard. Candles flickered on the table as we sat down. Antonio exclaimed, "So many stars!" as the sky darkened.

Platters of food made by cooks, who remained unseen, started to arrive from the kitchen. First came the freshly baked Focaccia, followed by pasta al pesto, seasoned tomatoes, baked artichokes, and salads containing everything except lettuce! Paolo's grilled fish was passed around with vegetables, which hid the fact that the fish was a bit dry but still flavorful.

"Emma, tell me about your friends!" Paolo asked as the pasta was being passed. Emma hesitated before starting to answer. I nodded to her and then intervened to answer Paolo's question. I told him I had been sailing since childhood and lived on the sea for about ten years. "Antonio here is like a brother to me; he and his wife and children are like family. We share our love of the sea and adventure. Antonio..." My friend broke in, being able to speak for himself. "I live in Salerno and run a boating business. Mostly tourists, sometimes private charter." Paolo nodded. "What do you think of Portofino?" he continued. Just as I was about to respond, his cell phone rang. He put his finger up to pause, took the call, and left the table. Emma looked at us and shrugged. "Business," she said.

After Paolo got up, an uneasy silence fell among the group. Emma and Gabriella eventually spoke up simultaneously; Emma motioned for Gabriella to share her thoughts. "I was wondering how you enjoyed your hike this morning. Besides meeting these two handsome men." Antonio and I laughed uncomfortably. "The sky was almost as blue as the sea," Emma began. "The water was so calm that it seemed like a sheet of glass. You could see a few fishing boats bobbing and the fishermen pulling up their nets. It was wonderful." "You always see so much, dear," Gabriella remarked. "Sometimes, maybe too much," Emma replied. Just at that instant, Paolo returned.

"Sorry," he said as he joined us. "I invested in a foreign company that may go under, so I had to decide whether to pull my money or not. It is a strange feeling", he continued, looking at us, "that we live in one of the most beautiful places in the world, and yet, at any instant, we could lose it. That's how the market is." "You would never lose everything; you are too smart for that!" Franco, one of the guests, exclaimed. Paolo laughed, then Franco continued, "What is that company? Perhaps I should disinvest also?" A conversation ensued on that side of the table about how to turn money into more money.

Emma looked at us and rolled her eyes. "Tell me about your adventures," she asked. "Have you two traveled together before?" Antonio glanced at me before answering. "This is our third or fourth trip together. Or is it our fifth or sixth? I don't remember. Before I got married, Gio and I sailed a lot. Once to the Greek islands. It was an amazing experience, right, Gio?" I nodded in agreement, not wanting to go into too much detail. "Then, another time, we sailed to the south of France to visit a friend of Gio's in Nice. He knows everyone! I loved that area but couldn't travel as much after getting married and starting my business. Sometimes, I stay with Gio in Brindisi during the off-season to give my wife a break," he said, chuckling.

"But isn't this sailing season?" Emma asked. I broke in here. "One thing you must understand about Antonio is that blood doesn't run in his veins, but seawater does. So it was time to set out on a sailing adventure because, from what I've heard, he was becoming tough to be around." Emma's eyes grew round in surprise. "Just ask his kids," I continued. Antonio laughed.

"Where is your family now?" Emma asked. "Enjoying some peaceful days with their grandmother in Sicily," Antonio responded. "Do you miss them?" Emma continued. Antonio thought a bit, then said, "No. I love my wife and my kids, but I realize I need time to let the seawater run through my veins, as Gio said. I am a better man if I take care of myself as well as take care of them." Emma nodded.

"But you asked about our adventures," I said. "Antonio, tell her about an adventure we had." Antonio looked at me and asked, "What about that time we picked up those migrants from Libya, then almost got arrested for it? Or when you forgot your passport, and we almost got detained in Morocco. Or, this is a good one," he said, glancing at Emma, "the time we were in Egypt and you met that beautiful woman. You took her to dinner, and then her father said you had to marry her!" Emma laughed, and I blushed.

"I can think of a few stories about you also, my friend," I replied. Antonio, in turn, blushed.

"OK, I will tell you one, not involving Antonio," I said, "since he doesn't want to be put on the spot. I will make a long story short and tell you about some close calls while sailing, especially when I got caught in a few storms." Antonio had heard these stories before, so I made it brief.

"Did you want to give up sailing after that? I would have," she said. "To be honest, after the first storm, I was scared. But because I was afraid, I did two things. First, I sailed again at the first opportunity because I didn't want to be ruled by fear. Second, I prepared better for longer trips. I researched, fitted out my boat with more supplies, and asked my friend Matteo to be my communication point when I was on the water for longer periods. So now, when sailing alone, he always knows where I am." Emma looked at me thoughtfully. "You have some good friends," she said. I glanced at Antonio and replied, "My friends are my family." Antonio shoulder-nudged me.

We savored dessert and coffee as we shared stories, and time passed quickly, seeming like mere moments. At some point, we became so engrossed in our conversation that we didn't notice the others getting up to say goodnight and leave. We quickly stood up and thanked our hosts and guests for an incredible evening.

Emma walked us to the front gate and asked, "Will I see you two tomorrow?" Antonio looked at me as if I had decision-making power. "Yes," I said. Emma had the morning planned already; "I can pick you up at the marina for breakfast, then take you on the most amazing drive of your life, apart from Amalfi, of course." Then she turned and called, "Paolo, can you come?" she asked. "I wish I could," he said, approaching us and shaking our hands. "I will see you at 9," Emma said as we left.

A driver was waiting for us outside their gate. We were relieved we didn't have to trek down the hill at night. We both went straight to bed when we returned to the boat. I slept soundly; before I knew it, the morning light called me to start the day.

Emma kept her promise and arrived in a red convertible. Antonio and I were amazed, and we jumped in, laughing. "It's like a Fellini movie!" exclaimed Antonio as we sped off.

We drove up the hills from the marina and arrived in the less touristy town of Camogli after a few minutes. We pulled up in front of a grand hotel next to a cafe. "Ciao Emma!" greeted the attendant as we got out. "Breakfast?" he asked her, smiling. "Grazie, Carlo," she responded as he motioned us towards an outside table.

It was a relief to be away from tourists. Camogli is a lesser-known town in Liguria with a livelier

31

fishing industry than other towns. We enjoyed our coffee, the view, and the cool air without interruptions. "I could get used to this," Antonio said. When I raised an eyebrow at him, he quickly added, "With Giovanna and the kids, of course!" Emma smiled.

"What do you have planned for us today?" I asked Emma.

"Do you want me to tell you the details, or do you want to be surprised and make it an adventure?" I liked Emma's style. Antonio and I replied, "Adventure!" and clinked our coffee cups.

We spent the remainder of the day exploring other areas around the Cinque Terre and even ventured into Levanto by a backroad that Emma knew. Nobody mentioned the previous evening or Emma's reference to being unhappy throughout that beautiful day until Antonio opened his big mouth.

As the sun set, we enjoyed aperitifs at a cafe with an incredible view above the Portofino marina. The world seemed perfect as we looked out and savored our drinks while reflecting on our experience. "This has been an amazing day," I said. "To Emma, our amazing guide," Antonio added. "Guide and friend!" I said as we clinked our glasses together. "I am also grateful. To be able to taste a bit of adventure in this beautiful place, which always feels the same," Emma said.

"I'm sorry that you're sometimes unhappy," Antonio said. Emma looked at him and then at me. "I'm not unhappy," she said calmly. "Just not completely happy. We all want a piece of what someone else has. Many would want the life I have. Part of me longs for your life, Gio, on that boat. Then, another part wants Antonio's life, with a family that always has him in mind. So, maybe my situation isn't different from others. It's times like these, with you, that help me realize that life is bigger than what I have. Yes, I long for more; I long for a husband who..." She didn't finish the sentence.

Perhaps Emma was right.

Whether it is the loneliness I sometimes feel on my boat, the longing that sometimes weighs on Antonio, or the feelings of dissatisfaction just around the corner from joy, happiness always feels incomplete.

As Emma looked at us, she smiled and said, "This is a special moment. Three friends sitting in Portofino, watching the sun transform the sky, reflecting on life, happiness, and love. This will be a memory I cherish forever."

The following day, as we continued our adventure up the coast and into French waters, I couldn't help but think back to that moment with Emma. Perhaps Antonio was thinking the same thing when, later that evening, as he stared at the sea, he suddenly exclaimed, "Isn't life amazing?"

# Chapter 3
# Sex in Santorini

The last time I was in Santorini was when my
relationship ended.

Maria and I had been in a long-distance
relationship for three years, as she lived in Spain. We
saw each other in person every four or five months.
We had planned to spend two romantic weeks
together in Santorini, but I didn't realize it would be
our last meeting.

Before she arrived, I felt uneasy. Over the past
year, Maria had hinted that she wanted something
more, which I wasn't sure I could provide.

I sailed to the island, and she flew in from
Madrid.

We made love when she arrived on my boat, and
I wished the moment could last forever. After
spending hours in bed, I asked if I could show her
something beautiful. She smiled, and I mentioned
my dinner reservations on the edge of the caldera,
where the sunset created a breathtaking view. We
needed to be there by 7:30. Maria smiled, kissed me,
and went to take a shower, promising she would be
ready in ten minutes.

# Onward

Fira is the busiest town in Santorini, where cruise ships dock and unload their passengers, and trinket shops are bustling with business. Even though it might not be the most beautiful town on the island, it's convenient and offers stunning vistas. I had made a reservation at a restaurant with views and an exceptional seafood menu.

Maria's dark eyes widened as we entered the restaurant terrace to sit down, the sea spreading out before us. The waiter brought us a chilled white wine, filled our frosty glasses, and waited for our approval. I gave him a thumbs-up, and he left.

"Wait," Maria interrupted as I reached for my glass again. "I want to capture this moment," she added, pulling out her phone and taking pictures of the beautiful sea view through our two wine glasses. We raised our glasses, clinked them, and smiled at each other. "This is amazing!" she exclaimed. "You always take me to the most incredible places," she continued. I smiled, took her hand, and replied, "You deserve it; you deserve all the memories we create together."

The waiter returned and handed us the menus. He then asked if he could share their specials and began listing them in accented English. As he went through the dishes, Maria and I caught the exact words at the same time. "Grilled octopus!" we both exclaimed. The waiter chuckled, went through some side dishes, and left us to ourselves and the magnificent view.

As we sat waiting for our food, Maria grew quiet. When the waiter finally brought our perfectly grilled seafood with fresh tomatoes, sliced cucumbers, and grilled fennel, I tried making small talk, but Maria seemed detached. After we enjoyed our meal and were served dessert, she finally spoke up and said she had something on her mind. She asked, "Gio, how are we doing?" Her question caught me off guard. "I think we're doing just fine, darling. We're the same as we've always been. But how are you doing?" Maria took a sip of wine and looked out at the sea. "For me, the tough part is the 'same as we've always been' part. That's what's been bothering me. Is what we have now the same as what we'll have in the future, or is there something more?"

I leaned back in my chair and gazed into Maria's intense eyes. I shifted my attention to the sea, trying to collect my thoughts. "The answer is simple - things might always stay the same. You know my life and how much I can offer," I replied, turning to her. She interrupted me and asked, "But would you ever consider relocating to Spain? We could have a home together, start a family, and you could still sail whenever you want." She paused momentarily and continued, "We are not getting any younger. What we have is beautiful, but we are not children. I hope there comes a time when we will have a life together."

Maria was expecting a different answer than the one I had given her. I didn't want to hurt her, nor did I want to deceive her, so I took a deep breath, paused, and reflected. Maria noticed my hesitation and urged

36

me to speak my mind. "Please, Gio, just say what you think," she said. I turned and looked into her eyes. "I can give you part of my life, but not my entire life."

Without warning, she stood up from the table and knocked over a glass, causing it to shatter on the floor. Several patrons turned their heads towards her direction as she leaned forward and spoke in a hushed tone, "I have given you so much, yet received so little in return! You are a selfish little man who thinks he is a great explorer, adventurer, and world traveler. You are nothing but a pathetic imposter who desperately tries to be someone you are not. You act like a child, a despicable one at that."

Then she stormed off.

I sat there, stunned. Suddenly, everything that was beautiful fifteen minutes ago was ugly.

I was confused about what was happening between us. We both understood the limits of our relationship since I had been living on the water when we met. We enjoyed one another when we were together and thought about each other when apart. But suddenly, everything changed. I was baffled.

I sat there thinking for a long time. I cared for Maria deeply, but I wasn't willing to give up the life I had built for myself. I didn't want to make promises I couldn't keep, and I knew that if I did what she asked, I would eventually resent her.

I couldn't think of words to say that would make her happy.

Maybe she was right; perhaps I was childish. But I knew what kind of life I wanted.

I decided to avoid the marina and instead strolled around the caldera, passing by tourists, shops, and restaurants. I wanted to avoid another confrontation, so I walked for hours past midnight. However, since I couldn't sleep on the streets, I had to return to the boat, secretly hoping she wouldn't be there.

As I approached the cabin door, I noticed it was slightly open. I crept into the sleeping area and found Maria lying on the small sofa, leaving the bed for me. She was facing the wall, pretending to be asleep. I didn't disturb her and quietly removed my clothes, crept into bed, and closed my eyes, also pretending to sleep. I even altered my breathing to deceive her because I didn't want to have any discussion about our relationship.

I could almost hear her say: "So, are we going to talk about this, or what?"

The night felt like it would never end, but finally, morning came. Maria got up first and left while I stayed in bed, weighing the situation with one eye open.

If our relationship was over, then there was nothing more to say. Continuing the discussion would only add to the pain and hurt. I was ready to move on and put this whole thing behind me.

I got out of bed, showered, and decided to find a cafe for coffee. Maria was nowhere to be seen.

# Onward

After breakfast, I wandered around Fira, hoping to avoid running into her. I stumbled upon a chapel and sought refuge inside. Later, I strolled down from the caldera and explored the rest of the town, eventually coming across a small park. I found a tree and lay down. Feeling lonely, I decided to call my friend Matteo.

"I know you, she knows you, and we all know what changes and what doesn't. The way you live your life won't change, my friend. Maria knows that, so you haven't done anything wrong. You never deceived or promised her anything you couldn't give. She's angry; let her be angry. But how are you doing, my friend?" he asked.

How did I feel? I was shaken and sorrowful and complained, "I hate this! I don't want to be here! I hate that she is hurt and angry!" Matteo interrupted me, "This will pass, my friend. Remember that lovers come and go, but friends remain."

"Thank you, brother," I said and hung up.

I avoided returning to my boat for as long as possible, but as evening approached, I had to face reality. I felt like a coward as I crept onboard. My heart sank when I heard Maria below as I descended the stairs. She must have heard me because she stood there with her arms folded when I got below deck.

"Can we please talk about this?" she asked.

There was nothing to discuss, but I didn't want to be cruel. "Yes," I said, sitting on the edge of the bed.

Maria sat down beside me and began to cry. I reached over and held her as her tears turned into sobs. "I love you so much!" she said, choking up. "I love you too, my Maria," I replied. I truly loved her but was unwilling to change my life. "Do you love me as much as I love you?" she asked. "I love you, Maria. I always have," I said. She continued to cry and sob for several minutes, and then suddenly, she seemed to be okay.

"I'm glad we had this time to talk. So we are okay now?"

Although I was confused about what she meant, I agreed we were okay.

"So you will be willing to compromise and move to Spain or have me move to Brindisi and start a family?"

My spine stiffened at these words. She must have sensed it as she insisted, "Are you? Will you?" I turned to look her in the eyes, not wanting any of my words to be misconstrued. "Maria, I love you, and that is true. However, I will not change my way of life. I will not move to Spain, and I will not move you to Italy to start a family. That is not the life that I want."

She searched my eyes for any glimmer of doubt or hesitation. She pulled away from my arms when she found none and stormed out.

As I sat there, I was unsure about my next step. I decided to give Maria space and time to figure out what she wanted. In the meantime, I went online and found a cheap place to stay for the night. Since I had no idea about Maria's state of mind, I discreetly secured my valuables and essential belongings, packed an overnight bag, and left for the lodging I had found.

I slept little that night, wondering if I had unwittingly set any expectations for Maria. I was also anxious about my boat and whether I could trust her. I woke up before dawn and went to the marina to make sure everything was secure. Then, I quietly returned to my inn and waited until the morning when I could get some coffee.

I woke up at 7, made some coffee, and forced myself to eat breakfast. I then passed the time until later in the morning. When I returned to the marina and sat where I could see my boat, there was no sign of anyone onboard. After almost an hour of waiting and watching, I decided to be the man, go on board, and confront the situation.

Finding nobody on the deck, I descended the stairs and heard nothing. I checked the sleeping area, but Maria was not there. I noticed that her belongings were gone, and on the nightstand, there was a piece of paper with a message that said, "I am sorry it has come to this. I left for Spain." As I read her note, two emotions flooded me: pain and relief.

I haven't heard from Maria since.

I didn't want to always remember Santorini in terms of that sorrowful breakup, so a few years later I sailed back to the beautiful island, hoping that new memories would cancel out old ones.

I decided to dock in Oia instead of Fira this time as it was said to be less crowded by cruise ship tourists. It was a beautiful morning when I arrived, and I was excited to explore the town.

I went directly to the blue domes of the Agios Spyridonas and Anastasios churches, which are beautiful monuments to the human spirit. I wanted to see them before they got crowded with visitors later in the day. I was not disappointed. I sat down on a ledge from which I could see the two churches with the Aegean Sea as their background. According to my research, they look ancient but date from the mid-1850s. The architecture, domes, walls, and the sea created a perfect view.

As it was Sunday, I tried my luck and checked if the churches were open. One was busy with services, but the other, named 'Anastasios' (meaning "Resurrection" in Greek), was empty. I walked in and was amazed by the floor-to-ceiling icons on gold backgrounds. Usually, I'm not a big fan of gold decorations, but this church drew me into a different world. I sat down to take it all in. As time passed, I felt like I had entered Oz without the Wizard. Everything looked, felt, and smelled different from the outside.

I felt like I could leave my problems, concerns, and worries at the door, become one with another presence, and then return to daily life.

The sun was so bright when I came out that I had to shield my eyes. I felt lighter, as if, somehow, I was able to leave my sorrow over Maria there. I slipped on my sunglasses as I strolled around the quaint town. The beautiful whitewashed and pastel buildings spilled down the side of the caldera, with a windmill or two in the distance and the ruined castle in the foreground. It felt like I was walking through a fairytale.

At lunchtime, the crowds began to show up, and I was repeatedly bumped and jostled, quickly making the town's magic wear off. I changed directions and headed towards Ammoudi Bay; the 300 steps to the water would keep the day trippers away.

I tightened the straps of my small backpack and continued walking. It was a rocky area with little sand but popular with swimmers and cliff jumpers. When I reached the cliff area, I saw a fishing village below, dotted with taverns and cafes. I decided to descend later to watch the sunset and avoid some of the crowds. But first, I found a spot to lay my things, stripped off my clothes to my bathing suit, asked someone to watch my stuff, and then ran to the cliff. I wasn't foolish enough to jump into the unknown, so I paused to see what others were doing, calculated the safest area to make the jump, backed up, ran, and then flew into the Aegean.

"Amazing" cannot describe the experience. As I hit the water, it was almost like being baptized: all of the regret, sorrow, and painful memories surrounding Maria were washed away. I felt complete and absolute joy and freedom. I laughed. I splashed. I was grateful.

After spending the afternoon in the water, except for an occasional cliff jump, I decided to head towards a tavern to watch the sun descend towards the horizon. Although I smelled of seawater, most people in town did too. I bribed the waiter with a heavy tip to get a good table and ordered appetizers. I wanted to enjoy a long, peaceful dinner, so I started nibbling on Dolmades (Stuffed Grape Leaves), Marinated Greek Olives, Fava dip with pitas, and a glass of sparkling wine.

To fully enjoy the sunset, I asked the waiter to wait until after it was over to take my dinner order, which he happily obliged.

The seafood was excellent, but the wine was mediocre. However, the views were breathtaking. I wanted to share my amazement with someone, and the only person nearby was a middle-aged American woman wearing a lot of makeup. I asked her, "Have you ever seen such an incredible sunset?" She sipped her wine, glanced at me, then at the horizon, and replied, "Isn't it breathtaking?" After a moment's hesitation, she introduced herself as Linda. I told her my name was Jovanny. We then shared our experiences. Linda was on a cruise ship that had docked overnight and chose to stay on shore to enjoy the sunset. She mentioned her husband, who remained on board the vessel; she emphasized that he was not on shore with her. She then shared the stops on their cruise, which seemed boring to me: jumping from island to island for tourists who wanted to get a glimpse without really understanding. But I kept this thought to myself.

Like many people I met, Linda was fascinated when I shared my stories about life on a sailboat, including the near misses. She asked, "What is the worst thing that happened to you?" and "Where have you not been yet that you want to sail to?" However, one question changed the course of our conversation: "What is the downside of living your life on a boat?" Until then, I had never given it much thought. Whenever I was done with a place or situation, I sailed on to the next or returned to Brindisi. But then I thought of Maria, which was certainly a downside. I pondered momentarily, looked at Linda, and replied, "Romantic relationships." She nodded, thoughtfully examining my eyes. "Well," she said, "I hope you don't believe marriage is the answer to all your romantic desires because it's not." I chuckled. "That's what my married friends say, too." Linda laughed.

As our conversation continued, it became clear that Linda was seeking companionship. "Where are you staying?" she asked. When I told her I slept on my boat, she mentioned that her hotel was just fifty feet from where we sat. "I will return to the ship in the morning, but the evening is mine," she said. I impulsively asked her, "Would you like some company back at your place?" Linda smiled, nodded, and asked the waiter for her bill.

As we strolled towards her hotel, I asked myself what I was doing. This woman was not someone I was typically attracted to. I probably would not have noticed her had we passed on a street. But I hadn't had sex in longer than I choose to admit, and this was an opportunity. It was the sex that attracted me, and I think it was the same for her. This was an opportunity, a blip, to be enjoyed, completed, and then forgotten.

Though I tried to enter the hotel discreetly, the clerk behind the desk looked up and studied me. Under his prying eyes, I followed Linda into the elevator.

Once in her room, passion took over, and the drive for sex made up for any other lack. She seemed to want it as much as I did. Perhaps she and her husband didn't have sex anymore? Or maybe it was exciting for her to be with a stranger. It didn't matter as I tore into her as she coaxed me on.

The time with Linda was neither a quickie nor an all-nighter. We spent three or four hours together until we were both fulfilled, spent, and smiling. "I should get back to my boat," I said. "Thank you," I added and kissed her. We both got dressed, and I prepared to leave.

There were few words between us at this point. We both knew nothing would be drawn out from this, no keeping in touch or attaching meaning. It was sex, for sex's sake.

When I was about to leave, she said, "I hope you continue to enjoy your adventures." At this, I kissed her on the forehead, said goodbye, and left.

## Onward

I walked past the cafe and then to the beach. It was past three o'clock in the morning, and the place was empty.

I climbed the cliffs again, stripped naked, and jumped into the sea.

As I floated in the warm waters, I gazed at the stars and smiled.

# Chapter 4
# Memories of the Nile

I hate flying, but when my friend Sadiki invited me to sail down the Nile with him from Luxor, I had to make a decision. I considered sailing to Alexandria and traveling overland to Luxor, but after plotting the route, I realized it would be too challenging. I had to fly.

I sucked it up, called Sadiki and told him I was coming.

Sadiki, his wife Masika, and I were close friends. Like me, Sadiki was passionate about the water, and his family had a long history of sailing the Nile. He owned a felucca, a traditional sailing boat that typically carries tourists down the Nile for a few hours or days. These boats are usually basic, with no running water or bathrooms. However, Sadiki's boat was different. He had modified it, making it more comfortable and convenient for longer journeys.

Sadiki created a business model to attract wealthier customers and, thus, achieve a better work/life balance. He refurbished his father's felucca, installing a bathroom, shower, and full kitchen. He kept the boat well-maintained, with immaculate white sails and a white hull with black and chrome detail. It was and is a beautiful historical craft.

Before meeting Sadiki, I was friends with Masika, who would later become his wife. Masika's father is Italian and from Puglia, while her mother is Egyptian and was born near Luxor. The family used to rent a boat on Sundays to spend the day on the Adriatic, stopping for lunch at coastal towns. One day, I met the whole family while cleaning my boat at the Brindisi marina. Masika's brother, Karim, asked how much it would cost to take the family out. I laughed and said, "I don't do this for money; I live on my boat!" The whole family gathered around me, asking questions. I invited them onto my craft, and we spent half the day together; I even showed them how to sail. Masika wanted to try, so I let her maneuver and demonstrated how to control the sails. Her brothers teased her, but she put them in their place.

This initial meeting led to a long-lasting friendship. We have shared meals at each other's homes and spent many Sundays together on my boat. We are like family, and Masika's mother has even started to nag me about getting married.

The family would visit her mother's relatives in Egypt every year, and during one of these trips, Masika and Sadiki met and started seeing each other.

A few months after they met, Masika's father, Nicola, asked me, "Gio, I want you to get to know this

Sadiki. Let me know what you think!" I thought he was joking but realized he was serious when he said, "Please, Gio." I suggested inviting Sadiki to stay with me for a few weeks to get to know each other. "That is an amazing idea, Gio. Thank you," Nicola said as he shook my hand and patted my shoulder.

A few weeks later, I heard a knock on the door and opened it to find a man of medium height and build with green eyes, a black goatee, and a well-groomed appearance. He was wearing shorts, a T-shirt, and sandals. "Mr. Jovanny?" he asked. "Mr. Sadiki?" I replied with a smile and shook his hand. I then showed him to the guest bedroom and helped him with his suitcase. "Thank Ra!" he exclaimed as he entered the room.

In the following days, I realized how unique Sadiki was. He firmly believed in ancient Egypt's gods and was highly knowledgeable about Egyptian history. His passion for his culture and heritage was so intense that he would sometimes get carried away, and I had to ask him to slow down. "Which god are you talking about now?" I would ask, making him pause, laugh, and then continue.

On the other hand, Masika had been brought up Catholic, but she didn't seem particularly religious.

I used to call her "my California girl" because she looked and acted like a tomboy from California. She had light brown hair and hazel eyes and had a tattoo on her shoulder of the Egyptian symbol of life (the Ankh) between two pillars, representing Egypt and Brindisi.

# Onward

When I first met Masika, I thought she looked like some of the volleyball players I had seen in Malibu. She was extremely athletic and was always off playing soccer, volleyball, or some other sport. If she didn't start speaking Italian, one would swear she was from Los Angeles.

She was always full of energy and up for an adventure, while Sadiki seemed more cerebral to me. Would this relationship work?

I forged a bond with Sadiki a few days later when we departed from Brindisi in my boat. We set sail in the morning and ended up far from the sight of land. The warm and gentle waves tempted us to jump in, so I furled the sails, and we did just that. Although water is my home, Sadiki was more of a fish than me. He swam around, under the boat, in circles, and away, never seeming to tire. I did a few laps around the boat and tread water until he returned. "Isn't this beautiful, Jovanny?" he asked. "Yes, it is," I replied, climbing into my small raft to relax. "I think we will be good friends," he added. "I think so, too," I said. Sadiki then took off to swim around the boat again. Our enduring friendship began in the waters of the Adriatic.

At the end of the week, Nicola asked, "Well, Gio, what do you think?" After knowing him for such a short time, I could not summarize a man's character, so I chose my words carefully. "Sadiki seems to be a good man, passionate about life and his Egyptian heritage, and he seems to love your daughter.

Masika, as you well know, is her own person. She doesn't like anyone telling her what she can and cannot do; she likes to carve her own path. They are both strong personalities and incredible people; there is no doubt about that. My only question is whether they can continue to be themselves and be together simultaneously."

Nicola nodded. "This is why I told Masika that there would be no talk of marriage for at least one year. Two is better. I have observed what you have, and I want them to have the best chance with no surprises if they marry someday."

I looked at Nicola, an older, tall man with a dark beard, a bit of gray, and dark eyes. I chuckled and asked, "Did you have any surprises after you married, my friend?" Nicola rolled his eyes and then smiled. "Yes, that is why I don't want them to go fast!"

During the second week, Sadiki shared some Egyptian hieroglyphs on parchment while revealing some personal information about himself. "My parents raised me Muslim, but it is all the same. I honor Allah, Ra, and the Christian God; they are different names but the same God. What is wrong with that? Now look at this symbol here, Gio. Do you see? It is called Ka. When I die, the Ka lives on like the soul. The sun is where all life comes from. Do you see this symbol? It is called the Eye of Ra. From Ra comes all life, warmth, and light. Do you see how Ra and Ka are related?" I nodded, staring at the hieroglyphs on the parchment he was pointing to. "I made this and want to give it to you," he said, handing me the parchment. "It is a reminder that Ra watches over us and that you are my brother, and I am yours, no matter what happens between Maskika and me. Will you accept this?" I nodded.

The parchment still hangs on my kitchen wall.

Though I am not shy about sex, Sadiki made me blush a few days later in another conversation. He shared his take on masturbation in somewhat awkward English. "When I reached puberty, I realized I could fuck my hand. But everyone said, 'No, it's a sin!' and 'If you do that, you will be punished!' or 'You will go blind!' I didn't believe any of that. It is a great gift, so why not use it?"

I held up my hand and said, "Too much information!"

He was on a roll and told me about his romantic relationship with a woman from Cairo. As he began to delve into the intimate details, I raised my hand again and interrupted him. "Stop, stop, my friend! I don't want to hear the specifics; you should keep them to yourself!" Sadiki appeared confused. "Why? You will never meet her; you don't even know her name! I can share everything with you; didn't I say you are like a brother? But if it makes you uncomfortable, Gio, I won't continue. I apologize." I chuckled. "It doesn't make me uncomfortable...well, maybe it does. I'm not sure. Anyway, I understand the situation without needing all the details. So, what happened between you and her?"

Sadiki laughed and continued.

"Some families in Cairo, not all, but some believe they are superior to others, particularly those families with a long history in the city. Her family disapproved of me because I worked on a boat. So we broke up almost five years ago." I nodded, curious. "Did you love her? Do you still have feelings for her?" I asked. He shook his head. "I didn't understand what love was. I was attracted to her, and I enjoyed having sex with her, but if we had stayed together, she would have grown tired of my lifestyle. Once the initial excitement of falling in love fades, you must consider what you have in common. And we didn't have much. The breakup was for the best. Can we go sailing?"

His sudden request, unrelated to our conversation, made me chuckle. "Sure. When do you need to be back for dinner with the family?" He calculated in his head: "In four hours, at eight. Can we make it?" I gave him a thumbs-up.

I started feeling like I was spying for Nicola, so that afternoon, I told Sadiki about the plan to get him to come here and that Masika's father asked me if I thought Masika and he would be a good match. Sadiki laughed and said, "No problem; I have nothing to hide. I am who I am, and I cannot change that. Masika's family should find out who I am now rather than later." Later on, during our sail, I asked Sadiki, "So how is Masika different from other women you've been with?" He was about to jump into the water but paused to answer my question. He turned and said, "My friend, I know that Masika is your friend, your California girl, and I also know that her family trusts you. For my part, I do not pretend to be what I am not, to know what I do not know, or to play any games with people." Sadiki sat down in front of me. "I love Masika. What you ask is an excellent question. If I have loved before, how is this different?"

He stopped to consider, looking out over the Adriatic.

"I have never met anyone like Masika. She is fun, adventurous, and full of life! And yet, there is a deep part of her that I admire. I can see that she thinks and considers important things for a long time before speaking about them. I can honestly say that I am really into Masika, but I don't want her to choose me if that would change her. I want whatever is best for her. If she would have me for her husband and could be happy with our life, I would ask her tomorrow. But if she would not be happy, then no. It would be a big step for her because she would come to live with me in Egypt since that is where my business is." He paused, then added, "Who would be crazy enough to do that?"

After spending time in Brindisi, Sadiki spoke with Masika's father and expressed his feelings for Masika. They both agreed on a long courtship, and if they would marry, they would live in Egypt to carry on Sadiki's business. However, during the off-season, they would live in Brindisi in a house provided by Masika's parents.

All of this took place about eight years ago. Eventually, the two did marry; they now have two children, a girl and a boy, Layla and Youhana. Youhana is the Arabic form of Jovanny.

Besides being a mother, Masika plays on the women's soccer team in Brindisi, runs a tourist business, and manages short-term apartment rentals in Luxor and Brindisi. She also loves to sail with me and our friends.

Fast forward. Masika and the kids are in Brindisi with her parents for a few weeks while I head to Luxor. Although it is February and cold in Brindisi, this is the high tourist season on the Nile. Sadiki does good business, so I was grateful that he was able to block out time for our Nile adventure.

I had to change planes twice to get to Luxor, and by the time I arrived, I was feeling exhausted. It had been a long time since I had been in an airport, but the Luxor airport seemed chaotic, with security guards, employees, tourists, locals, and a mixture of everything in between rushing around. Eventually, I found the baggage claim sign and followed it until I heard my name, "Gio!"

A minute later, Sadiki was there, hugging me and crying. He always cried when we met up or went our separate ways. I am used to it now. But when he started crying the first time I picked him up at the airport in Brindisi, I thought I had said something to hurt his feelings. When I asked him, he cried even more. "I am so happy to see you, my brother!" He always makes me emotional when he sheds tears.

Sadiki took my suitcase, and we got into his car. "Where to now?" I asked. "First, we'll rest. Then, tonight, we'll go out to see something incredible," Sadiki replied.

I was too excited to sleep, but a few hours of relaxing after the flight did me good. When the sun had set, Sadiki took me to dinner, where we toasted our friendship and destiny. "I want to show you something that you must experience at night. It will be the first step on our adventure," he said as we set out.

Sadiki took me to a temple area on the other side of town. As we approached the entrance, we saw two enormous statues of Ramesses standing as guards. Sadiki greeted the statues by bowing and said, "Greetings, Ramesses. Welcome to the temple of the dead." His eyes were glowing with excitement as he led me to a specific destination. I followed him, admiring the over 3,000-year-old columns. The stones spoke louder than the tourists talking, chatting, and pointing.

"Why the temple of the dead?" I whispered as if we were in a church. "Because, like all of us, Ramesses wanted to live forever. Besides having his body mummified, he wanted his memory preserved among his people. So here, surrounding us, is the temple that proclaims the connection between the pharaohs and the world of the divine. It is where the two worlds, human and divine, converge."

We stood still, side by side, gazing up at the stars between the columns.

"Come," said my friend as we continued our journey back in time. "I want to show you those who sought to live forever, each leaving their mark." We entered what felt like a chapel, and Sadiki motioned for me to stand beside him as we looked at the carvings. "There you see Alexander the Great, dressed as an Egyptian Pharaoh; his name is inscribed in royal Egyptian cartouches here," he said, pointing. "Now we are within the convergence of Egyptian and Hellenic cultures; we see the new ruler, Alexander, standing before Amun, asking for blessings and fruitfulness. We are inside the shrine of Amenhotep III, which was built a thousand years before the rest of the temple. Look, Gio, at the different eras of these images, and yet the message across the centuries is the same. In the face of death, we still yearn to live forever. We can see this in Ramesses, Amenhotep, and now Alexander, all in this place." After a few minutes, we moved on.

We next stood in the illuminated Hypostyle Hall as Sadiki got his bearings. Eventually, he turned to me and said he wanted to show me one particular spot in the Luxor temple —one spot that encapsulated why the temple was built. It was a place deeply meaningful to him and his life, and he wanted to share it with me before we embarked on our Nile voyage.

# Onward

We entered a room and found a place to sit next to a wall. Sadiki sat beside me as we looked at the frescoes facing us. "What do you see?" he asked. "I see faces," I replied. "Yes, but more," he insisted. I looked at the bigger picture. "Well, on one side, you have carvings that depict life in ancient Egypt and the life of the pharaoh, just like the rest of the temple. But then, on the left, you can see that part of the Egyptian hieroglyphs has been plastered over, and on top of them, there are painted faces. These faces are of people who are all looking in the same direction. I think they are Romans," I concluded, satisfied with my observations.

"Now," my friend whispered, "what does it mean?" I didn't answer because I knew he wanted to explain. Sadiki was born to be a teacher. "Which part of this fresco is missing? I'll give you a hint. In the Coptic period, this area was used as a church." I leaned back against the column and looked at the scene. I could count eight men with eyes fixed on the same object, which was no longer visible. "Well, if it is a church, it must be..." I hesitated, comparing the images to others I've seen in ancient churches. Suddenly, it came to me. "Christ, they are looking at Christ, and that part of the fresco is missing!" I finally said triumphantly.

Sadiki patted me on the back and then stood up, using his gestures to direct my gaze. "Now, Gio, pay attention," he whispered. "Why are they looking at Christ? What do they want?" I looked at the fresco, then at Sadiki, and finally shrugged. He gestured towards the painting. "They're seeking the same thing that Ramesses sought, that Alexander fought for, and that you and I are here for!" He paused, his eyes shining in the dim light. "ETERNITY! They're all seeking eternity. And that's why we're here, Gio. Right here, in this place, all three cultures of Egypt, Greece, and Rome converge. We are in that sacred place where longing and fulfillment meet. Isn't that incredible?" Sadiki said, emotion in his voice. I stood up and joined him, gazing at the fresco, the hieroglyphs, and recalled the figure of Alexander.

"I love this place," Sadiki began as he leaned against a column, tears welling up in his eyes, "because it is my life. I am from Egypt, and I have all my history and traditions. Masiki is from Brindisi. Even though she is half Egyptian, she is more Italian in her mentality. She is like this fresco, with all her history and traditions. But these are not in conflict; they form something beautiful together, like this fresco next to these hieroglyphs. It is beautiful, isn't it?" I nodded my head in agreement. "But who is the Greek part of the fresco, then?" I asked, smiling. Sadiki laughed and replied, "That is you, my friend. Always seeking, always sailing, but never quite arriving. Yes, Gio, that is you," he said, putting his arm around my shoulder.

We remained silent for a long time in that place, under the stars and the faint sounds of tourists in the distance.

We both felt a sense of being part of something greater within the Luxor temple. When we finally left, it was as if we had taken a piece of Luxor with us.

We boarded Sadiki's felucca early the next day. The two-mast sailing ship is designed for the comfort of about eight people, and the design dates back to the ancient world. We were sailing on a river of history onboard a vessel descended from the time of the pharaohs. Yet Sadiki's felucca was all decked out with state-of-the-art facilities and sparkling clean. He charged higher rates than others, but his clientele was loyal, and he thus avoided the "Can you take me out for an hour?" crowd. Sadiki made more money on longer voyages and always provided the best possible experience to his customers, who would then spread the word about his excellent service.

I stepped onto the boat, took off my shoes, and stood on what appeared to be a large bed. "There are two levels," Sadiki explained, watching my expression. "Many like to stay on the upper level to see the shores, the river, the sky. But the Egyptian sun gets hot, so we all end up down here. This floor," he explained, motioning with his arm, "serves as a bedroom, living room, and dining room. Let me give you the tour," he said, leading me forward. He then showed me the kitchen, stocked with a vast quantity of food for us, followed by the small onboard bathroom and tiny shower. When I mentioned that I could bathe in the river, Sadiki warned me against it, saying that swimming in the Nile for foreigners was like drinking the water in Mexico – risky and potentially vacation-ruining. The Nile contains bacteria that foreigners may have no resistance to, he explained. "Stick with the shower, my friend." Sadiki knew I loved the water and could see I was unhappy. "We will stop and moor the boat every night, Gio. Along the way, I have some friends who manage hotels with pools. We can swim there." Although it wasn't the same, I gave him a thumbs up.

Since feluccas have no motor, we relied on the winds, which perfectly suited me. "It's the journey that's beautiful, Gio," Sadiki said as we gently sailed towards Aswan in the middle of the Nile. "Look, Gio! You're sailing on the river where Cleopatra laughed with Caesar, Ramesses floated by his monuments, and the great pharaohs admired their kingdom. You're here. Can you feel it?" he said excitedly. I laughed and looked around. "Yes, I can feel it."

That night, I was captivated by the same stars that once fascinated historical figures like Nefertiti, Tutankhamun, and Amehotep. The sound of the waves lapping against our felucca felt like whispers from a distant past. I must have dozed off, because, before I knew it, I opened one eye to see Sadiki sitting beside me, holding a cup of coffee. "Are you going to sleep all day, Gio?" he asked with a smile. "What time is it?" I questioned. "It's 6 o'clock. Don't say a word, Gio! We want to get to the Temple of Horus before the crowds arrive!" I sat up and took a sip from the steaming cup.

Once I was up, we had a hearty breakfast, freshened up, and got ready for the day. After reaching Edfu, we docked our boat and walked through the town, which felt like a trip back in time. Donkeys, carts, and worn-out cars were everywhere. However, we had a goal in mind and soon found ourselves in front of the temple that had been standing for over 2,000 years.

"I am overwhelmed," I said as Sadiki pointed towards the temple. "This is not the most ancient temple in Egypt," he said, "but it is the best preserved. Do you see the walls around the temple, Gio?" I nodded, and Sadiki continued, "They acted as a dam to protect the temple from the flooding of the Nile. But before we go inside, tell me what you think?" The temple was enormous, and the people coming in and out looked tiny. The inscriptions, carved figures, and statues were so perfectly preserved that I was speechless. "Gio without words; now that is a novelty!" Sadiki said, laughing.

We took a few steps forward.

Sadiki asked me, "Gio, do you see the figures of Horus, the Falcon god, around the entrance? What do you think of him?"

"I think he looks like a creature from a horror movie," I replied. Sadiki made a face and continued, "My friend, what does it mean? These are just stones unless we discover the meaning."

I looked at the entrance but could only see a falcon head on a man's body. Sadiki could tell that I was puzzled. He suggested, "Let's go over in the shade for a minute, Gio."

I followed him, and he bought a few bottles of cold water from a nearby vendor and gave me one.

"Each animal possesses a unique gift that allows it to survive and thrive. A dog has its sense of smell, a turtle has its shell, and a whale has its size. But what about the falcon? What is its gift?" This one was easy. "His eyesight," I replied. Sadiki exclaimed, "Yes, my friend! The falcon's eyesight! It can soar above the earth and spot prey and predators from a great distance. Now, look at Horace. He has the head of a falcon, not because he is a monster, but because he is a protector. He guards humans using his keen sight to identify friends and foes and anticipate potential threats. Horus can see things that we cannot, including hidden evils. Therefore, he is the symbol of protection, and his eye became known as the 'eye of Horus.' Does that make sense to you, Gio?"

We arrived at the entrance, and Sadiki asked me to look up. He began explaining the meaning of our journey down the Nile. "To your right and left are the two banks of the river. But above your head, way up, you see the sun disk of the great god Amun Ra. Now, on each side, you see cobras. Do you see them, Gio?" I squinted and managed to spot them.

Sadiki continued, "The key to this temple is the eye. Cobras cannot close their eyes, and I believe that is true for all snakes. But, for the ancients, the cobra held special significance. The eye of the cobra that you see above your head tells us that Horus's eye is always on us, and he never sleeps. His protection is always available for those who seek it. So this eye, the eye of the cobra, of Ra, of Horus, watches over Egypt on both sides of the Nile and watches us too."

He paused, chuckled, and asked me, "Now that you know the story, does Horus still look like a monster?" I laughed and replied, "Yes," to get on his nerves. Sadiki playfully punched me in the shoulder and said, "Come, my friend."

We walked through the first hypostyle hall and then to a smaller space called the Appearance Hall. As we went forward, the atmosphere got gloomier. "Are you scared, Gio?" Sadiki asked, laughing. I stopped and hid behind a pillar until I heard Sadiki call my name. Then I crept behind him, grabbed his arm, and made him cry out. We both laughed.

I smiled and asked Sadiki, "If Horus can see everything, why is his temple so dark?" He replied, "Because he sees what we cannot. Gio, have you ever noticed the symbol of an eagle in some Christian churches?" I paused, but Sadiki continued, "It is the same idea: the eye of the eagle, the eye of the falcon, the eye of Horus."

We stood silently in that chamber where priests ministered and Pharaohs begged for protection.

As tourist groups started to arrive, we left and stepped out into the scorching sun. I had to shield my eyes because I felt blinded. "There is a legend that only the eagle can look directly at the sun," Sadiki explained. "That's why you'll often see the eagle symbol in churches, and here you can find the falcon," he added.

We wanted to avoid the crowds of tourists, so we left the area and made it to our felucca just as a large hotel boat was docking.

As we continued our sail, the images of what we had just witnessed filled my imagination.

"I'll make lunch if you can steer the boat, Gio," Sadiki offered. So, we took our positions and got ready for another fantastic afternoon.

After we had finished eating and relaxed for a few hours, we watched the sun starting to set. We were peacefully gliding toward Aswan.

The sun reflecting off the water seemed magical.

Sadiki was lying next to me, observing the shores pass by. We saw communities that have remained unchanged for thousands of years, fishermen on feluccas, modern buildings, and noisy motor boats.

"How do you think the cult of Horus compares with other beliefs?" I asked Sadiki. He looked at the sky as he reflected; I could see some birds circling high above. Then he responded, "In some Christian churches, the eagle symbolizes St. John, who wrote the fourth gospel and the Book of Revelation. He had visions before his death and could see things that others couldn't. It is the same concept with Horus, the falcon, the eagle, and the visions of St. John. They can see everything because they have two eyes. They look at death with one eye, and with the other, they look at life."

The sun slipped behind the horizon as Sadiki added, "I am a happy man, Gio, because I think of death daily. And because I think of death, I can steer my life to a happy place, to a good destination."

"Just like us right now," I replied.

"Yes, my friend, just like us."

We eventually arrived at Aswan and witnessed the beauty of the temple of Isis, Abu Simbel, and other remarkable sights before returning to Luxor.

However, even after all these years, our visit to the temple of Horus in Edfu has remained etched in my mind.

My friendship with Sadiki and Masika reminds me that keeping one eye on life and the other on death means life is short and a gift.

The temple taught me not to take anything for granted, especially friendship.

# Chapter 5
# Catastrophe in Catania

I sailed to Sicily years ago to explore its rich history and culture. I visited the Greek theater in Taormina, Ortigia in Syracuse, and the baroque town of Noto. Now, I wanted to discover what Catania and Palermo had to offer.

Since the boat docking fees in Catania were affordable, I decided to make it my base and head to Palermo the following week.

My decision to go to Sicily was at the last minute, so I lacked some supplies. Upon docking in Catania, I was in no mood to hunt for provisions or to begin cleaning my boat, so I farmed out these tasks to the men at the marina, leaving them a list of supplies and instructions, along with payment.

I left the dock area and headed towards the center of the town. I soon found myself standing in front of the majestic cathedral; the dark volcanic stone of the church walls spoke of the origins of the rock from which the city was made. Turning around, I saw Catania's symbol - a dark gray elephant statue believed to have originated from the Roman Empire or possibly even before. This stone animal has been the official symbol of the city since the 1200s.

The air in August was hot, baking me and the tourists who had filled the central piazza. Despite the heat, I was determined to explore the city and wanted to get a sense of it before visiting any specific site. Therefore, I decided to take a leisurely walk down Via Etnea, the main pedestrian street lined with expensive chain stores and dingy shops.

In 1693, a devastating earthquake hit Catania, almost destroying the city. As a result, most buildings that currently stand were built in the 1800s. During my walk along Via Etnea, I couldn't help but notice that many of these buildings have been restored and now house large stores, which gives the city an elegant and sophisticated appearance.

However, I was interested in exploring a more authentic side of Catania and decided to venture outside of the tourist areas. As I walked off the beaten path, I noticed that block after block, building after building, were dilapidated 18th-century palaces that barely seemed to hold together. These structures appeared to have not been maintained or updated since they were built. The electric wires were hanging perilously on metal clamps, the rusted balconies were sagging under the weight of several generations of junk, and no fresh coat of paint was in sight. This gave me a different impression of the city that lost its glory long ago. It felt as though neglect and corruption had become the norm.

As my stomach began to growl, my attention shifted from admiring the buildings to searching for food. I didn't like these dilapidated streets, so I returned to the commercial zone on Via Etnea. I stumbled upon a cafe where I ordered a tourist menu consisting of stale rolls, cheese, and salty cold cuts. To accompany the meal, I also had a watery Aperol Spritz.

Although the food could have been better, the people-watching was exceptional. The crowd mainly consisted of tourists, including groups of students from the United States, AirBnB guests hauling their luggage, German visitors conversing and pointing, and a few Italian sightseers leisurely strolling. However, there had to be more to Catania than just this. I longed to explore the city further to experience its vibe.

The area's most impressive building was the cathedral, so I went back to the beloved elephant, passed street performers, navigated through groups of tourists, avoided beggars, and stepped into the shade of the church. Several young men were stationed at the entrance, barring tourists from entering as Mass was about to start. "Messa?" one of them asked me. "Si," I replied. He stepped aside and gestured for me to enter.

I took a seat and looked around. Was I here to pray, observe, rest, or meditate? I decided to do all four. It had been ages since I attended a Mass, so I was open to reconnecting with the divine.

I recently read about the cathedral's reconstruction after the earthquake in 1693. The original structure was completed in 1093, but I saw no evidence of this ancient history in the baroque design from where I was seated. As I looked up at the ceiling, I expected to see heavy, gold leaf decorations everywhere, but instead, it was a refreshing bare white plaster.

The church was cross-shaped and had an altar area dripping with gold-covered figures. However, something drew my focus away, and I found myself gazing at an almost Art Deco-style fresco of St. Agnes being crowned in heaven.

Does God really spend time putting crowns on people who lived holy lives? After all, a crown is just a piece of metal to which humans attach meaning. How many boxes of these crowns exist in heaven to be placed on the heads of saints as they enter paradise? And if humans become spirits once they die, can they be awarded a physical crown? Does God even believe in crowning people?

These thoughts passed through my mind, and I couldn't help but chuckle.

Then, the priest walked out.

I looked around and noted a handful of older women and some devout tourists who sat in the central nave while other visitors, who had managed to bypass the guards, were wandering around in the side aisles as the service began.

"In the name of the Father...."

I looked around, up at the ceiling, the priest, and then the fresco. I decided to participate and followed with my sign of the cross.

I found the tourists on the sides distracting, and my mind wandered. But still, though my thoughts were elsewhere, something about being in that space gave me a sense of peace.

As the priest started preaching, I tried to learn something meaningful from his message. However, he began with a vague reference to the Gospel, then started complaining about how our society has become secular and how fewer people attend church. He then discussed an upcoming festival and went off on another unrelated tangent. I looked around the congregation and noticed that everyone seemed disconnected. As he rambled on, I couldn't help but glance at my watch and grimace when I realized that he had already been speaking for twenty-five minutes with no sign of stopping. On and on he went, as congregants tried to listen politely and children squirmed. "Will this ever end?" I whispered to myself. Should I leave, I wondered? Time passed, my annoyance grew, and then suddenly, he concluded. Forty-five minutes of preaching about…I don't think any of us knew.

But this was my moment, and I wouldn't let it be taken from me by a stray sermon. "Why am I sitting here?" I asked myself.

I was there because I was grateful for my life so far.

# Onward

This thought helped me regain a sense of peace as I sat, looked, and reflected.

When I left the cathedral, dusk was approaching, and I decided to grab some food supplies for the boat. On a side street, I discovered a grocery store for tourists, where I found pasta, water, coffee, and fruit. I loaded everything in a few large bags and left.

It was dark outside, and I noticed a large empty apartment complex across the street built in the past few years and spanning several blocks. A few units had lights on, and a big sign stated that apartments were available for rent.

Despite some hints of elegance, I couldn't help but feel that Catania was a failing city as I walked through its non-touristy streets. I passed many houses that were up for sale, buildings that looked dilapidated, crumbling streets, and piles of garbage.

However, as I had just arrived, I wanted to learn more about the city before forming a firm opinion.

Returning to Via Etnea, I crossed the cathedral square and turned on a street towards the marina.

I boarded my boat, dropped my bags on the deck, and looked around. I hoped it would be clean, but it was clear that none of the maintenance I had paid for had been done. I had foolishly prepaid someone at the marina to clean and restock the cupboards below, but none of the supplies I had ordered had been delivered and it was as dirty as I left it.

I lugged my bags of supplies below and resolved to deal with all of this in the morning.

As I didn't want any adventures on my first night, I made pesto pasta on board and planned to take a walk later.

I took my steaming pasta and a bottle of wine, went up to the deck, and sat in a chair facing Catania. The city was illuminated, highlighting its historical wonders and downplaying its defects. As I sat there, I began to relax and enjoy the view of Catania from afar. Around 11 o'clock, I raised my glass, toasted the city, and decided to go to bed.

The next day, I was excited to explore some of Catania's history. I had two sights in mind: the Benedictine monastery and the second-century theater.

What was once a sixteenth-century monastery of monks of St. Benedict is now the home of the Humanities Department of the University of Catania. I arrived around 8:15 and signed up for the Italian tour, scheduled to begin at 8:30. I found a spot to sit in the courtyard, which provided me with a good view of the students coming and going. Although excited about the tour, I felt tired since I hadn't slept well. Something about Catania made me uneasy, but I couldn't pinpoint it yet.

During the tour, I learned that the monastery was established for the local aristocracy. This monastery's monks focused more on food and comfort than prayer and work. The guide explained that the Benedictine monastery was crucial in Catanian society. It provided a place and purpose for sons of noble families who were not the firstborn and, therefore, not entitled to inherit. Many of these monks were not naturally inclined towards religious life, but they still gained prestige in the city by following the monastic routine.

The food facilities caught my attention as we navigated between groups of students and explored the buildings. One notable structure was the "Coffee House," which stood in the center of the abbey and served as a place for the monks to relax and enjoy hot chocolate or liquor. Later, we visited the monastic kitchen and saw a large barbecue dominating the room. These monks didn't adhere to the typical vegetarian one-meal-a-day regimen common in other monasteries.

During the tour, a visitor asked about a rumored tunnel between the monastery of monks and the nearby nunnery. The guide dismissed this as folklore and said no tunnel had ever been found. Furthermore, monks who wanted to have a mistress wouldn't require a tunnel.

The monastery's history was fascinating, but without any monks present, the place felt somewhat empty. I was ready to move on and didn't want to do another tour, so I decided to skip the theater and go to the beach instead.

I took it as a good omen that private and public beaches populated a boulevard named after a U.S.

president: Viale Presidente Kennedy. However, I wasn't sure which beach to go to, so I hailed a taxi and asked the driver to take me to the free beach.

A few minutes later, as we drove along Kennedy Boulevard, I was scanning for a spot where I could be dropped off. Both sides of the streets were lined with parked cars along dozens of unappealing private beach entrances. Cheap-looking plastic signs and billboards invited visitors to come in and pay a fee to relax among the tackiness. When I finally spotted a free beach, I exclaimed, "Yes! This is perfect!" After paying for the taxi ride, I quickly got out, walked across the street, and across the sand, dodging little kids, food baskets, and elderly ladies. The water looked like a bubbling soup filled with floating human-shaped croutons.

This place would not do.

I walked along the shoreline to a neighboring private beach. There was loud music, a dance floor with few people, and crowds lounging on rented chairs and lounges.

This place would not do either.

I left the beach and walked along the main street, hoping to find a better area. A sign for 'America Beach' caught my eye, so I approached it. However, I found the same level of tackiness as before, so I decided to move on.

Out of stubbornness, I checked out even more beach locals, but they were all alike. Tacky, crowded, dingy.

# Onward

Eventually, I decided to call it a day and took a cab back to the marina. I spent the rest of the afternoon on my boat.

I had a few more days left in Catania before heading to Palermo. After the beach experience, all I wanted was a good dinner, a great glass of wine, and some friendly conversation. So, I asked around at the marina, scolded them for not cleaning my boat yet, got a few café tips, and took off.

I have a tight budget and don't usually splurge often. However, after consuming seafood for weeks, I strongly craved steak. Following a suggestion, I found myself in a fancy restaurant in the historical center crowded with tourists. I wasn't concerned about authenticity; I simply wanted a great steak.

"Table for one, please," I asked in my smooth Italian. "Where would you like to sit, sir?" the waiter asked. I chose a table for four with a good vantage point to people-watch. "Excellent, sir," the waiter said as he handed me the menu.

I ordered a bottle of Brunello, a rare steak, and tried to explain to the waiter what a baked potato was. I had to settle for "patate al forno," baked with rosemary and olive oil. I leaned back to enjoy a quiet evening. I removed my man purse, rolled up my sleeves, and released a third button on my dress shirt. The wine made the moment almost magical.

Although the steak was a bit tough, the potatoes were excellent, and the tomato salad was great. Luckily, the Brunello redeemed it all.

I sat contentedly, sipping the last drops of wine and enjoying a slice of tiramisu while observing the passersby. I asked the waiter if I could settle my bill and stay longer. "Certainly, sir," he responded.

As I leaned back in my chair, I took in the bustling scene of locals and tourists walking by. Suddenly, a voice interrupted my thoughts. I turned to see a striking woman with long black hair, green eyes, and a dress barely containing her ample bosom. She was sitting alone behind me to the left.

"Excuse me," she said. "I couldn't help but notice you switching between English and Italian. I was wondering where you're from. I'm from Catania, but I learned English in an American school as a student."

I turned towards her, my gaze falling on her breasts; her face and eyes remained a mystery when I looked up. "I was born in California," I responded. "But now I live in...many places." She smiled and scooted closer. "It sounds like you have an interesting life. Is this your first time in Catania?"

With all the small talk, I wasn't sure if she was flirting with me or just being friendly. I asked her why she was alone, and she replied that her friends had planned a night out together, but one got a cold, another had a sick child, and the other couldn't make it. So she decided to take herself out for a nice evening. I nodded. "Yes, the same with me, except for the friends. I don't know anyone in Catania." "So you are here alone?" she asked innocently. I nodded. "Then it is very nice to meet you. My name is

Giuliana," she said, shaking my hand, holding it longer than a casual handshake.

Giuliana talked about her friends, life, and love for Catania and asked to show me the city the next day. "That would be wonderful," I said.

Suddenly, she looked at her watch and stood up. "I'm sorry, I have to go. Would you like to come with me?" I paused, considering the situation. "It was very nice meeting you," I replied. "Could you at least walk me to my street?" she insisted. "Where do you live?" I asked. She proceeded to give me a messy set of directions. "I'm sorry, Giuliana, I can't do that. I have to leave myself. Good evening." With those words, she departed, and I never saw her again.

The restaurant was closing, and I needed to return to my boat. So, I quickly gathered my belongings and headed towards the cathedral square. I turned down a side street and headed to the marina.

About an hour after leaving the restaurant, on my boat, I discovered that my wallet was missing. As I emptied my man purse and laid out all my belongings for the next day, everything was there except the wallet.

I might have dropped it on the street or left it at the restaurant. So, I started to retrace my steps when I received a text message asking if I had authorized a charge of 950 euros at a bar in Catania. It hit me that my wallet had been stolen and that the thief had used my credit card. I immediately refuted the charge.

It dawned on me that I had been taken for a ride. I foolishly left my belongings on the table as I turned to chat with the pretty lady. Her accomplice must have reached over, took my wallet, and left the bag so I wouldn't notice. Her invitation to accompany her was also a part of this scheme. If I had accepted, things could have played out even worse.

It didn't take long for me to panic. I searched for my passport, keys for the boat engine, house keys, and cell phone. Thankfully, they were all still there. However, my driver's license, two credit cards, a bank debit card, and about 150 euros in cash were gone.

I told myself to calm down as I felt myself choking up. First things first: cancel the credit and debit cards. I got on the phone and blocked them all.

"Can I get a new card sent to me?" I asked the credit card company. "Yes, you should receive it in ten to fourteen days," was the response.

I could not pay the docking fees, fuel, or other supplies. The panic returned and I didn't know what to do.

Feeling overwhelmed, I sat on the bed and thought about my friend Matteo. He would know what to do in this situation. However, I felt ashamed and stupid for finding myself in this predicament. I didn't want anyone else to know about it, so I decided to solve the problem independently.

As my panic increased and confusion about what to do overwhelmed me, I made a U-turn on my previous decision. I decided to put aside my shame and ask for help. Finally, I texted Matteo, "Somebody stole my wallet in Catania, and I don't know what to do. Please call me."

Matteo called immediately. "Gio, what happened?" I was stammering and upset, trying to explain that I had put my wallet on a table and turned around, only to find it missing. Matteo reassured me, saying, "Don't worry, Gio, we will find a way to help you. I have a friend in Catania who travels often for work. If he's in town, I'll ask him to loan you the money to return to Brindisi. I'll contact him now and get back to you. Just try to stay calm."

While waiting for Matteo's reply, I reviewed the evening's events step by step.

I started to beat myself up. "You are so stupid!" I told myself a hundred times. There were multiple hints during the evening that something wasn't right. Her interest in a stranger, engaging in meaningless small talk, her sudden request for me to walk her home. What was I thinking? A pretty face, bulging breasts, and all my caution flew out the window.

I began to realize that I am not the sophisticated world adventurer that I want to believe myself to be. Instead, I am just a stereotypical naive and foolish American who made myself a target. Stupid. Stupid. Stupid. I am so stupid, I repeated incessantly.

I looked at the things on the table that hadn't been stolen. If my passport, boat keys, boat, or house keys in Brindisi were gone, I'd be in deep shit.

I remembered the feeling of peace in the cathedral, which seemed like years ago.

Suddenly, a text arrived. "Gio, I heard back from my friend. Just by chance, he is in Catania tonight, not far from the marina. He can loan you 250 euros to get you back home; then you can wire him the money. He can be there in an hour. Does that work for you?" "Yes, yes, yes. Grazie. Grazie. Grazie."

I was done with Catania. I had no desire to stay another minute. I got online and arranged to dock in Brindisi.

I waited outside for Matteo's friend, who arrived about forty-five minutes later. I reassured him that I would wire him the money when I got home. "I don't know how to thank you," I added. "Don't worry, send it whenever you can. Just keep safe," he replied. He was a good man, just like Matteo. After paying my docking fee and filling the backup tank with fuel, I jumped on my boat.

Fifteen minutes after I received the money, I pulled out.

The water shimmered under the full moon as I sailed away from Sicily, but the scene's beauty did not move me. I kept replaying every moment of that evening, analyzing my choices, distractions, movements, and words. Each time I failed to notice what was happening, I berated myself for being naive and deceived. I called myself stupid over and over again for hours.

Matteo called me and asked, "Gio, how are you doing?" I replied that I felt like a fool. He tried to comfort me by saying, "Gio, my brother, don't worry.

# Onward

This happens to everyone. I had a similar experience when I was in Milan years ago. Don't be so hard on yourself." Even after I kept repeating how stupid I was, he continued to assure me I wasn't.

My self-confidence was shattered. I kept questioning myself, "What is wrong with me?" I couldn't believe I even considered living on a sailboat. How could I possibly navigate new places and interact with different people and cultures when I couldn't even spend two days in Catania without getting robbed?

These thoughts kept beating up my mind, making me feel helpless.

But then I stopped. I asked myself, "Would I treat my best friend like this? Berating them for hours over a mistake they made?" The answer was no. I asked myself, "Then why am I treating myself like this?" I tried to imagine how worse the situation could have been, which helped me realize that even now, I had something to be grateful for.

I arrived at the Brindisi dock at dawn and made it back to my house a few hours later. "Did you arrive safely? Do you need anything?" Matteo texted me. "Grazie fratello - thank you, brother," I texted back. "I am so grateful for you. Now I am going to bed."

Ten hours later, I woke up.

I decided to lay low for a few days while I waited for my replacement credit cards to arrive and my shame to subside.

My self-confidence was low during the following days that stretched into weeks, and I didn't want to see anybody. "Where are you, Gio? Are you OK?" Matteo would text. "Yes, just resting," I lied.

After two weeks of this, I realized that I was falling into depression and that I needed to take action.

I couldn't control my feelings, but I could control my actions. I decided to stop isolating myself and have "smart feet."

I called Matteo and invited him to go fishing. I anticipated he would bring up the situation in Catania, but he didn't. Some other friends joined us, and as we grilled fish on the beach, I expected everyone to ask me what happened, but they didn't.

These bonds of friendship brought me back to the present and made me realize that making mistakes is a normal human quality.

I am greater than my mistakes.

What are some of the lessons I learned from this experience? Besides the obvious ones, like not leaving my wallet unattended on a table, being cautious of overly friendly strangers, and not trusting someone I do not know, there are others.

I need to stop being so hard on myself and treat myself like my own best friend.

Some friends who are like family have earned my trust and affection.    Mistakes are the path to wisdom.

# Chapter 6
# Love in Dubrovnik

I was in my twenties when I sailed into the marina near Dubrovnik for the first time. I had been living on my boat for just a few years and felt I could conquer the world.

Little did I know that I would be conquered.

Her name was Lori—a simple name for such a unique person.

I had been planning this sail for months, as I was fascinated by the area's people, culture, and history. I intended to spend a week exploring the city before continuing inland and then along the coast.

As I caught sight of the medieval walled city, my heart began to race. The rocky shoreline was peppered with small, sandy beaches, and the surrounding walls protected the orange roofs of the medieval quarter. It was as though the city was beckoning me to join its beauty.

I had planned to stay in the city for a few nights, rent a car, and then venture into the countryside. I wanted to see what I could discover without relying on guidebooks or tourist itineraries.

Once I had docked my boat, paid the fees, and secured it, I inquired about a guest house. The marina staff suggested an American woman who ran a small bed and breakfast in the historic center.

They gave me directions, and I set out.

I lugged my duffel bag and passed through the gate but soon found myself lost in the winding streets of the old city. I tried to follow the directions, but they led me to a market. Then, I used my phone for guidance, but it only led me in circles. Eventually, I started asking around and zig-zagged through almost every ancient street until I finally found "The Croatian Sunset." The sign had a miniature painting of a sun setting over waves and a small surfboard, so I knew I was in the right place.

The large wooden door looked freshly varnished, the surrounding stones were gleaming white, and the street was away from the tourist path. I rang the bell, and a female voice from the speaker greeted me, "Good morning! Can I help you?" I explained who I was, why I came, and what I needed.

There was a buzz, and then I was inside.

I stood in a large room with a vaulted ceiling, stone floors, and a wall of windows facing a garden. I heard footsteps on the stairs and turned to see the silhouette of a young woman descending in front of a large window.

"The marina sent me here and told me that this is the best place in town for me to stay," I began. "I'm from the US, have money, and am not a serial killer."

She laughed and replied, "I can see you're from the US, but I'm unsure about the other two."

"Well, I guess you'll have to take a chance," I said, extending my hand. "Jovanny. I plan on staying a few nights here in Dubrovnik if you have a room. If not, I can sleep on my boat."

She introduced herself as Lori and led me over to the check-in desk.

"Things are not busy now," she said, "you're my only guest. In a few weeks, things pick up. So, yes, the room is yours. Here are the rates. If that works for you, I'll take down your information."

I handed her my passport and credit card. As she recorded my information, I looked at her more closely. Lori seemed about my age, with long blond hair, blue eyes, and slightly freckled. She looked like a combination of a movie star, rock climber, and surfer.

"Do you surf?" I asked as she continued typing.

"Back in California, at least twice a week. These aren't surfing waters, but I still paddle out. What about you?"

"I used to surf in Malibu. The last time I surfed was in Senegal, which was amazing."

She laughed and then looked up at me curiously as if she just had some realization. Then, she bent down to her computer and completed the transaction.

"I usually jog along the city walls in the evening. The views are incredible, and it's the best way to get an overview of Dubrovnik. You're welcome to join me if you don't have any plans," she said. I nodded and replied, "That would be great, but let's walk today and maybe jog tomorrow?" Lori smiled and replied, "Sure, see you at six!"

A few hours had passed, and we found ourselves gazing down at the stone buildings with orange-tiled roofs that make up the city and the gentle waves of the Adriatic on the other side. That evening, only a few people strolled along Stradun, the main street in the center. We continued walking towards an overlook and leaned on the wall to enjoy the view of Lovrijenac and Bokar Fortresses, with the translucent blue harbor below and the town spilling along the cliffs. Lori climbed on the wall and sat, facing the castle, while I leaned out and looked at the water. I asked, "Why did you come here? And why do you stay?"

Lori glanced at me, then turned and replied, "You know why I came here. You are looking at it. As for why I stay, I wanted a bigger life than the one I had in California. But nobody was going to hand it to me. I had to be creative. So I researched, studied Croatian, got a degree in business, and bought a one-way ticket here. That was five years ago. Why do I stay? Because for the first time, I am living the life I want instead of the one everyone wanted for me."

She paused, then asked, "Does that make sense?" I nodded. "It makes a lot of sense," I said. Lori laughed.

"My family, especially my parents, don't think so. They think I'm crazy."

"That's because they don't understand what a bigger life means," I replied.

Lori hopped off the wall and led me to a cafe just a few steps away. "Would you like something to drink?" she asked. We ordered two glasses of chilled white wine as the sun began to set. After taking the first sip, Lori asked, "Can you tell me more about your story?" "It is similar to yours but with different circumstances," I responded.

"Details," she said.

As I shared some life stories on a sailboat, Lori seemed to understand my motivations even before I finished. "Without our dreams, we would not have this," she said, gesturing towards the sunset over the water. "I understand why you stay," I said, looking into her eyes. Suddenly, she stood up from the table and asked, "Shall we?"

We continued our stroll.

It took us a few hours to walk the length of the walls around Dubrovnik. As we approached the inn, I wanted our time together to continue. "How about dinner?" I suggested. "I know the perfect hidden gem," she responded as we turned around and walked up some stairs across a cobblestone street and into a medieval-looking alley.

As we entered through a nondescript door, the proprietor greeted us warmly, saying, "Hello, Lori!" She replied, "I have another convert for you!" Lori replied. The owner, a short, round, black-haired Croatian man in his fifties, shook my hand and welcomed us. "Welcome, welcome, welcome," he repeated.

"Why is he so happy to see us?" I wondered. "Lori, I have some fresh fish caught this morning. It is out of this world! I can grill it for you with just a bit of olive oil and lemon and serve it with a side of Blitva (fried potatoes and chard) and some of the freshest tomatoes you will find in Dubrovnik. Then, a glass of white house wine from my brother's vineyard would be the perfect match. What do you think?" he asked her.

"Perfect as always, my friend," Lori replied.

"Vinko" was the owner's name, and he didn't lie. He served the most delicate white fish, Sea Bream, fresh tomatoes, salad, blitva, fresh crusty bread, and chilled white wine. "This food is incredible; why don't more people know about this place?" I asked Lori, looking around at the empty tables. "Because I like to keep my favorite things secret," she replied without skipping a beat.

Perhaps it was the wine, the end of the day, or the companionship, but we both felt relaxed and on the same page. When Lori spoke, I listened attentively. When I spoke, she listened with interest. And when neither of us spoke, our thoughts seemed to run parallel.

# Onward

At a certain point, Lori noticed I was smiling and asked why. "I'm just happy to be here, I guess," I replied. Looking at me, she added, "Me too."

As we sipped our wine, I thanked Lori for a beautiful day. She reached over and clinked glasses. I had never felt so comfortable with a woman before; usually, I felt like I had to keep the conversation going, come up with exciting stories, or try to be funny. But with Lori, it wasn't like that at all.

When we were leaving, Vinko approached our table, shook my hand, and kissed Lori on the cheek. "Come back soon, my friend!" he exclaimed as we walked onto the street.

As we approached the inn's door, I felt myself becoming increasingly nervous. I was attracted to Lori, but I didn't want to do or say anything that would make her uncomfortable. She unlocked the door and gestured for me to go inside first. "Guests first!" she said with a smile before turning the bolt from the inside.

"I have an early appointment with a plumber tomorrow," she told me as we entered. "So I am going to wish you good night." With that, she gently leaned in and kissed my cheek before disappearing down a hallway. I stood there at the bottom of the stairs, watching her go. "What an incredible woman!" I whispered to myself.

That night, I had trouble falling asleep because something was bothering me about Lori. Although I was strongly attracted to her, I couldn't quite put my finger on what was troubling me. I felt both happy and scared at the same time.

After struggling to fall asleep for a few hours, I decided to go to the kitchen to get some water. I tiptoed down the creaky stairs, trying not to wake Lori, whose room was just down the hall. When I opened the fridge, I heard a voice behind me say, "So you couldn't sleep either?" It was Lori, looking beautiful as ever, sitting on the bar stool. "Nope," I replied. "Is the bed too hard or the room too hot?" she asked. "No, everything is perfect; that's why I can't sleep," I responded. She looked at me curiously, and it seemed like she understood what I was trying to say. "Nothing and nobody is perfect, but I'm glad you like it here," she said. "I wish..." I started to say but then stopped myself. "You wish what?" she asked. "I don't want to say. I don't want to ruin things," I said. "You might wish for the same thing I do," she replied. "Can I stay with you?" I asked. She got up, kissed my cheek, took my hand, and led me to her room.

From that night on, I slept in Lori's room every night.

I was overwhelmed with passion, unlike anything I had ever felt before. Our physical union made us feel connected on all levels.

Back then, I believed that love was destiny. The intensity of our physical pleasure and emotional compatibility convinced me that we were meant to be together.

# Onward

It only took me a week to confess my love to Lori; it took her even less.

When guests arrived the following week, I helped at the inn by making breakfast, checking people in, and fixing a broken dresser. As our lives became more intertwined, I felt extremely happy.

After spending a few weeks in Dubrovnik, I decided to call my friend Matteo and tell him about Lori, our chance meeting, the great sex, and the emotions that bound us. He listened attentively and asked, "What does this mean for you, Gio?" I paused and puzzled over his question. I was lying on my boat, so I put him on speaker and placed the phone on my chest so I could think. "I'm happy with her and want to be with this woman," I finally said. "I see," Matteo replied. "But what does this mean for your life? From what you are saying, you are living her life. What about yours?"

Why was Matteo not happy for me? His best friend found love, and he questioned me about it? I had expected a different reaction. "I have to go; call you back tomorrow," I said and hung up.

I was annoyed. I felt like Matteo had pushed me against a wall and wagged his finger in my face. "Fuck him," I muttered. I left the boat and returned to the inn.

Lori and I usually had free time in the late afternoons. We often went to one of the beaches, walked, or jogged on the walls. In the evenings, if no guests were checking in, we strolled through the winding streets of Dubrovnik, holding hands as we gazed at people, shops, and buildings. We chatted about our pasts, our hopes, and dreams.

After our walk, Lori and I made love again with as much passion as the first time. I felt grateful that fate had brought us together. However, later that evening, Matteo's words echoed, "What does this mean for your life?" I was initially annoyed with him, but I soon realized he was a good friend with every right to ask. The truth was, I didn't have an answer.

Matteo's reality check interrupted my sense of destiny. The next day, I felt bothered and shared this with Lori. She asked, "What does he mean?" as I recounted Matteo's words. She shrugged and said, "Isn't being together enough without making it into a plan?" I agreed but then proceeded to make a plan. "If I cancel the sailings that I have scheduled, it becomes a plan, whether we call it that or not," I said. "I have two sailings planned this month, one with Matteo and the other alone. After that, I can return." Lori smiled and said, "That is an excellent idea. We have each other, and I am here. But I don't want you to change your life for me."

When I arrived in Brindisi the next month, Matteo greeted me at the marina. "My friend!" he called out as I secured the boat. Although he knew my arrival time, I was surprised to see him there. Our last conversation could have gone better, and I had only texted him since. Matteo and I have been friends for a long time, and we did not want to jeopardize our friendship. "Can I buy you a beer?" he asked, and I agreed as I stepped out of the boat. He hugged me and kissed me on both cheeks, and we laughed as I said, "We will always be friends, Matteo, even when we have to tell each other things we don't want to hear!" Matteo laughed, too.

"My friend, your life is yours. I don't want to see you get hurt. I will always support you and want you to be happy, Gio. You know what is best for you."

I appreciated Matteo's words and our mutual honesty.

Over the next few weeks, I sailed around the Adriatic Sea multiple times, alone and with Matteo. However, my thoughts were filled with Dubrovnik even as I was physically out on the water. It was frustrating when I couldn't talk to Lori due to a weak signal. "You've got it bad!" Matteo laughed as we sailed out of Brindisi one morning. He was right.

Six weeks later, being back in Lori's arms felt like coming home. Her embrace was all I needed.

My life in Dubrovnik centered around Lori. We did almost everything together—worked, ate, slept, swam, made love, and then repeat.

During my time in Dubrovnik, I didn't keep in touch with Matteo or other friends very much. However, he eventually messaged me with a warning: "If you do not call me, you will die." So, I called him.

Matteo told me about the woman he was dating in Brindisi who would eventually become his wife. His budding relationship contrasted with mine. While I felt a sense of urgency, he expressed calm. Where I nurtured fears, he spoke of certainty.

The days turned into weeks, and I was in bliss until Matteo dropped another bomb.

At the end of a call, he said, "It's not like you to not keep in touch. It's as if, when you're there, you're living Lori's life; what happened to yours? Did you get swallowed up?" He chuckled.

Matteo didn't intend his casual comment to fall on me like a bomb, but it did.

When I was with Lori, I was the happiest. But when we were apart, I felt sad and scared that I might lose her. I had worked hard to build the life I had, but it started to feel like an obligation.

This realization made questions surface that I had avoided: to have a lasting relationship, would one of us need to give up the life we had built? Would I have to sacrifice my dream of a life spent sailing, or would she need to abandon her business in Dubrovnik? What kind of sacrifices would we have to make to be together?

I had no answers, only questions.

I spent a few months in Dubrovnik before returning to Brindisi. After only a few weeks, I decided to close my place and move in with Lori until the Spring.

I felt incredibly happy during those months, even though, by most standards, our daily routine was boring. We cared for the guests, maintained the inn, cleaned my boat, went grocery shopping, cooked meals, and enjoyed long evening walks. However, these mundane tasks felt magical because we were creating a life together.

Beneath the surface, there was a different story. I tried to ignore the turmoil in my mind. What would the future hold? What decisions would we need to make? What will happen in the Spring? Will I stay or go? Will she stay or come with me?

I wished I could enjoy our relationship for what it was in the present, as Lori seemed to be able to do, yet my mind raced when I tried to fall asleep.

A few months later, my friend Matteo came to visit. We avoided discussing my relationship over the phone, but I couldn't hold it in when he arrived. I needed to vent to someone I trusted.

I picked Matteo up at the airport and took him to a peaceful café outside the city center where we could talk. I shared that I was sure Lori was the most incredible woman I had ever met. I had never felt so embraced, understood, and loved in a relationship. I explained how our relationship had evolved, where it stood, and my thoughts and hopes for the future. I also shared my uncertainty about the next steps. "Are you in love with Lori?" Matteo asked. I smiled, nodded, and replied, "Never have I been so much in love."

Then, Matteo dropped a third bombshell.

"Just because you are in love with someone doesn't mean you are meant to be with them."

My mouth hung open. I was speechless. Angry, Outraged. Hurt. Sad. Confused.

Matteo continued, "I'm not sure what you should do, my friend. I understand that Lori is a great woman, and you are a great man. However, it seems like your life has been getting smaller and smaller since you met her. Your friendships, plans, and dreams are being pushed aside. It's not anybody's fault; it's just the type of relationship you have. You appear to be so afraid of losing her that you're losing everything else. I wonder if..."

Matteo paused for a moment. "If what?" I asked.

He continued, "I wonder if you've ever asked yourself a simple question." He stopped and looked at me expectantly. "The question is, my friend, whether this relationship is good or bad for you. I won't say anything more. You're my friend, and I care about you, and I'll always be your friend, no matter what you decide."

"Now," he continued, changing the subject, "show me this beautiful city."

Matteo spent a few more days in Dubrovnik, and during his stay, he, too, fell in love with the city. He and Lori got along well and seemed to like each other. But, after Matteo left, his words haunted me. He asked me the one question I had been avoiding: was my relationship with Lori good or bad for me? It was a difficult question to confront because I genuinely wanted, needed, and longed to be with her. But was this a good thing? I had to face it. I had to tell her what was in my heart.

A few days after Matteo left, Lori brought the whole matter up. "You have been sad lately, Gio. Why?" We were walking the walls of Dubrovnik and standing near where we had our first conversation. I sighed and looked at her and then at the beautiful vista. I was always honest with Lori and needed to speak my heart. "I don't know how to navigate being with you, building on what we have, and having my own life." I turned to her and continued, "When I am here with you, living your life with you, I am so happy. But when I leave to live mine, I am sad. Then, when I think of moving here to be with you always or you moving to Brindisi, I get confused. Neither seems like a good solution." Lori replied, "Aww, my love, you're always thinking about the future. Can't we enjoy what we have now and let the future unfold without figuring it out beforehand?"

Her words seemed reasonable. "Of course," I said and kissed her.

Looking back, I now realize that I began to conceal my emotions from Lori and myself from that day. I was determined to make our relationship work and was prepared to give up anything, including my mental peace, to achieve that goal. Whenever I was feeling unhappy, I refused to acknowledge it. Similarly, whenever I felt anxious, I convinced myself I needed to calm down, live in the moment, and try to be more like Lori.

I spent months in this state until my departure for Brindisi approached. Sailing season was about to begin, and I had made half-hearted plans to visit Albania and some Greek islands.

I had become accustomed to pretending to be the carefree and happy person who had arrived in Dubrovnik the year before. But Lori saw through it.

On the day before my departure, she cornered me in the kitchen. "Gio, I love you, and I know you love me. But you want more than I can give," she said. I tried to stop her, but she continued, "Let's look at our situation. You aren't going to give up your life to live here, and even if you were willing, I wouldn't let you. You would come to resent it. I won't give up my life to move to Brindisi. So, what do we have left? I see two alternatives: continue with our present situation or stop trying to be what we cannot. It is so painful to see you sad, Gio...."

I objected, "But I am not sad! I love you!"

Lori was determined to continue and put her finger gently on my lips. "I don't want you to think of me but of you. When you leave for these months, I want to ask you to think whether our situation works for you. If you can be happy with it or not. If you can, then return in the Fall. If you do not return, I will understand."

Then Lori dropped a bombshell herself. "You cannot be happy with me unless you are happy with yourself. You cannot be happy with my life unless you are happy with yours."

I left the following day for Brindisi.

# Onward

While sailing back to Italy, I felt like half the man compared with the one who first came to Dubrovnik.

Six months have passed without contact as I try to understand what happened. "You fell in love; then your relationship became more important than you. That never works. What is there to understand?" Matteo chided me. But why, I wondered. Was it something about Lori that brought out a neediness in me that made me cling to what we had at all costs? Or was this my emotional makeup in all relationships? Was I that pathetic that I needed someone else to be OK with myself?

After Dubrovnik, I began to rebuild my life. I planned sailing trips, spent time with friends, and sought new adventures. Focusing on my life taught me how to be content and at peace with myself.

I am grateful that I discovered love in Dubrovnik, but I don't know if I would be willing to pay its price again.

# Chapter 7
# Gaudí and Me in Barcelona

I've visited Barcelona many times since it is an easy sail and has an excellent marina. I usually came for the nightlife, beaches, and women. But I was looking for something different this time.

I have always enjoyed building relationships with people from the past and present. For instance, I developed a strong interest in Caravaggio and decided to follow in his footsteps in Rome. I visited his former residence, churches, museums, and other places associated with him to experience his art. It was my way of catching a glimpse of his spirit and getting to know the man. Over time, Caravaggio and I have become good friends. More recently, I also befriended Van Gogh, although getting to know him was a bit more challenging since his work is scattered worldwide, and his personality is pretty eccentric. However, after visiting Arles, where he was inspired, and Amsterdam, where many of his paintings are housed, we got to know each other well and built a strong bond. Now, I consider Van Gogh a close friend, just like Caravaggio.

# Onward

I have a strong personal connection with Barcelona because I have always admired Gaudí, who I consider a genius. Some people have commented that I resemble him, which has become a running joke among my friends. They often tell me that I look like a young Gaudí. Whenever someone comments on the similarity, I play along and claim that Gaudí is my great-great-uncle.

Although I had never really explored Barcelona's artistic side, I planned a trip to spend some time in the city with my "Uncle G" and leave the nightlife for another occasion.

Going to Barcelona to discover Gaudí would have an uncertain outcome. Would we like each other? Would we become friends? Would Gaudí inspire, frighten, or disgust me? I had no idea.

After securing my boat at the marina, I went to Casa Vicens, where everything started. I was eager to encounter the young Gaudí, fresh out of college, who wanted to establish himself in the architectural world. Gaudí was only a few years younger than me when he got his first major commission.

As scholars debate the influence of Moorish and Oriental styles on this architecture, I decided to avoid academic discussions and instead let Uncle Gaudí's work speak to me. I had no particular expectations but was hopeful I would catch a glimpse of the man through his work.

As I headed towards Carrer de les Carolines, I couldn't help but notice how unremarkable the neighborhood was. There were a few historical buildings and clean streets, but mostly plain apartment blocks, parked cars, a pharmacy, and uninteresting shops. There was nothing special until I glimpsed IT.

As I walked past an unattractive apartment building with graffiti-covered doors, I noticed one of the facades of Casa Vicens across the street. I stopped to admire the architecture and joked with Uncle G: "Gingerbread house with candy canes." My first impression of this house was childlike, joyful, and appetizing. But as I approached and gazed longer at the multi-level structure, I began to see more than just gingerbread.

Casa Vicens, a building completed by Gaudí around 1888, was his first big project. He wanted to make a statement, so he went all out on this building. The more I looked at it, the more details I noticed. What initially looks like gingerbread and candies turns into a whole garden scene with plants, water, sunlight, and birds. Before I went inside, I walked around the house to see what I could make of it.

As I walked around, I imagined what it must have been like in Gaudí's time when the area was still a countryside of fields, grass, and flowers. Unfortunately, the current concrete and asphalt landscape detracts from Gaudí's intended experience to create harmony between nature and Casa Vicens. In fact, it was the surrounding fields that originally inspired Gaudí's work.

"When I went to take the site measurements, it was covered with some yellow flowers, which I used as an ornamental theme for the ceramic. I also found an exuberant palmetto palm, whose leaves fill the house's gate grid."

I found the gate Gaudí described, which seemed more like a living thing than an entrance. The gate's design was not just a simple palm motif; the metal branches appeared to stretch out as if they wanted to embrace me. "This is amazing," I whispered.

I stepped back and crossed the street to better view the entire structure. The lower levels looked like a trunk covered in flowers, supporting the upper level, a burst of color, geometry, and flowering plants. I stared at the brownstone underbelly, which seemed to symbolize the earth, covered with tiles that echoed the colors and shapes of nature.

The house was once surrounded by Gaudí's carefully planned gardens, which mirrored the building's nature motifs. Sadly, the gardens no longer exist, as the land was sold to developers. Nonetheless, I couldn't help but imagine the beauty of the gardens and the architecture of the building, creating an incredibly harmonious combination.

From what I have seen, Gaudí had two goals. First, he wanted to celebrate creation with a joyful hymn in tile and stone. Second, he wanted to make a name for himself. At thirty, he was relatively unknown; this was his big opportunity to leave a lasting impression, and he definitely succeeded.

It was time to see what he would reveal to me inside.

"This is so cool," I exclaimed as I entered the dining room and gazed upwards. Nature was everywhere; the house structure seemed to be the vehicle through which nature's beauty flowed, with birds, flowers, and branches appearing to stretch out toward me. It was as though the plants and flowers were vying for space between the beams, competing to take over. His use of simple materials such as stones, tiles, paper mache, and paint was magical, as they combined to create a vision of nature that felt like paradise - like Eden but without sin.

I walked out onto the veranda that adjoined the dining room, where the interior and exterior met. Looking up, I saw a clear blue sky framed by palm branches, surrounded by yellow oriental-style shutters.

Every inch had something beautiful. Uncle Gaudí had a busy mind and seemed to have so much beauty to express that he couldn't find the space. So he filled every angle and surface that he could. As I continued walking through the house, I felt a sense of longing that the simple materials could not quite contain.

If I were to describe Casa Vicens in one word, it would be "bursting." The design was bursting with life, overflowing with the energy of nature and the joy of being alive. Gaudí's work expressed his discovery of beauty, and he tried to showcase it in his creations. The beauty was so immense, and his work was so small that life seemed to burst out from every beam, wall, and window.

As much as I enjoyed exploring Casa Vicens, it was time to move on and explore Gaudí's other creations.

Although he obtained the commission for the Sagrada Familia while still working on Casa Vicens, I decided to visit the church last since it was where Gaudí worked until his death.

My next stop was the Güell Palace, where Gaudí received a commission from a wealthy industrialist named Eusebi Güell. By this point, Gaudí had already established himself and didn't need to prove himself further. Casa Vicens was his resume; I remembered this as I walked towards the palace and looked up.

The word that came to mind was "sober." Gaudí's playfulness and joy were only visible on the roof, where the colorful ceramic chimneys contrasted with the seriousness of the architecture.

I wondered what surprises Gaudí had for me, considering the explosion of color and varied materials I had just seen at Vicens.

As I approached the entrance, I noticed two huge parabolic arch gates designed for horse-drawn carriages, topped with intricate, curved forged ironwork. The twisted metal in the middle formed a Catalan coat of arms that seemed to defy gravity, and I thought, "Here is my Gaudí." Though the color may not have been playful, the form certainly was. I felt relieved.

I hated waiting in line but trusted that it was worth it. After about fifteen minutes, I stood in the central hall, where Uncle Gaudí worked his magic. This room appeared to be the heart of the house, holding all its elements together. It seemed almost sacred. I felt like I was in a church as I gazed up at the soaring ceiling and heard the soft tones of the pipe organ playing above my head.

The space was dark, with even the three-story glass dome casting little light on the gray marble floors, columns, and dark wood where I stood. Beyond a massive door was an altar, almost consecrating the space. There was a progression from darkness to light: the stables below were cast in darkness, while where I stood was barely illuminated by shafts of light from above. I wondered what I would find as I walked up the stairs.

As I ascended to the highest level, the roof of the Güell palace, I felt as though I was on a spiritual journey. Like Dante's Divine Comedy, the palace appeared divided into three levels. The first level, the stables, felt like the darkness of the soul, where one struggles with feelings of sadness, confusion, and even depression. The second level, the central hall, was partially illuminated, offering a glimpse of the joy to come and prompting me to look upwards toward the light streaming from above. Finally, the third level, the sun-drenched roof area, was fully illuminated and revealed in all its glory.

# Onward

When I reached the top, everything made sense. The colorful chimneys exuded happiness, contentment, and a sense of arrival. It was clear that this was the final destination, the place we were meant to reach after traveling through darkness and symbols.

Gaudí's expression of the divine through stone and tile was mystifying and captivating. As I looked over the city he loved, I couldn't help but smile.

But it was time to move on.

I decided to leapfrog some of Gaudí's works, jumping from the completion of Güell palace in 1890 to his much later work, Casa Mila, completed in 1912. I wanted to get a broader perspective of his vision before I explored his magnum opus, the Sagrada Familia.

As I stood across the street from Casa Mila, I was welcomed by soft white ripples resembling the foamy waves from my boat heading towards the shore.

I knew a bit of the history behind this place, which represents Gaudí's unbound creativity. He felt so free that he even clashed with city officials for ignoring building codes and with the owner, the Mila family, for not following the budget limits. Gaudí's mind was too grand to be bogged down by the trivial things that most of us worry about.

Casa Mila meant greatness, creativity, daring, stubbornness, and conviction.

The Casa Mila, also known as "La Pedrera" or "the quarry," was initially mocked for its design. However, Gaudí had confidence in his unconventional vision and didn't let the negative comments affect him. Despite facing criticism, Gaudí was determined and seemed to know he was ahead of his time. Interestingly, Gaudí planned to install three religious statues on the building's roof – the Virgin Mary and two angels, Michael and Gabriel. Unfortunately, these statues were never installed, and this setback nearly led Gaudí to abandon the project. Thankfully, his priest friend convinced him to continue and complete the building.

As I stood looking up at the spaces where he intended his statues to be installed, I thought Uncle Gaudí's desire for religious symbolism in his creation hinted at where his heart and mind were at this time. The Sagrada Familia was becoming a reality, and he was already absorbed. But before heading there, I wanted to be inside Casa Mila to get a feel for the man during this part of his life.

I stepped into the central hall of Casa Mila and stopped in awe. It almost felt like I was in the middle of a jungle, surrounded by plant life crafted from paint, metal, and plaster. The rays of light surrounding and illuminating me caught my attention, giving the interior a floating sensation. Unlike the heavy feeling I experienced at Casa Vicens, this interior seemed to float on lily pads held by tree trunks and grass blades. It was as though a giant Alice in Wonderland might appear and ask me, "What are you doing in my house?"

I knew the roof was considered the most magical part of the structure, so I climbed through the jungle layers until I emerged into the sunlight. The atmosphere was completely different; I was surrounded by stone, plaster, and tile in a sculpture garden. I was standing on the "rooftop of the warriors," so named because Uncle Gaudí sculpted the chimneys and air ducts to look like stone soldiers peering over the city.

I didn't fully understand Gaudí's faith, but I could see hints of it in his work. Since he couldn't install his statues on the roof, he got creative and twisted some chimneys into crosses. One chimney depicts the letter "M" as a reference to the Virgin Mary. Another chimney featured a heart facing his hometown, which might express his yearning for the simplicity of his childhood.

I noticed a sad expression on one of the warrior chimneys. As I approached it, I saw the Sagrada Familia in the distance. The stone face seemed fixated on the church, and a tear rolled down its cheek. I wondered why. Did the artist somehow know that the creation of the Sagrada Familia would consume him so much that it would be his end?

It was time to leave this place and head towards the place that made Gaudí weep.

As I strolled through the streets of Barcelona, I couldn't help but reflect on a remarkable man who had once frequented them. He was talented and admired, always impeccably dressed, and played an active role in the city's social scene. In his younger years, he was a regular at parties and events in Barcelona's high society. However, a series of events led to a drastic change in his personality, turning him from a social butterfly to a solitary recluse who lived only for his work.

This change may have begun with Gaudi's experience of unrequited love.

The story of Gaudí's love life is complicated but more or less goes like this: Gaudí was deeply in love with a woman named Josefa Moreu, but unfortunately, she did not feel the same way. After this failed attempt at romance, Gaudí never fell in love again.

In the 1910s, Gaudí experienced a series of deaths that had a profound impact on him. Firstly, his father passed away, which caused him to fall into a severe state of depression. Then, his niece, whom he was very close to, also died. In 1914, his friend Francesc Berenguer passed away, followed by the death of Josep Torras. Finally, in 1918, his collaborator Eusebi Guell also died. This series of deaths must have shaken Gaudí to his core and led him to reassess his path.

Although Gaudí was always religious, he began to take his faith to a whole new level. He changed his social circle and started attending Mass every day. He even stopped buying new clothes. In some sense, he became the Sagrada Familia. This church expressed not only his craftsmanship but also his evolving vision of life.

Upon my arrival at Sagrada Familia, I felt sad. Gaudí, the famous and popular architect, had become a recluse to the point that people who passed him on the street didn't recognize him. He moved into a room at the Sagrada Familia to work there day and night, living a very simple life, eating little, and dressing poorly.

In 1926, Gaudí was hit by a tram while crossing the street. Bystanders assumed he was a homeless man and neglected his care for days. Eventually, someone recognized him in the hospital, but by then, it was too late for the doctors to save him, and he passed away.

These thoughts made me hesitant to visit the church that had taken the life of such a great man. I admired Gaudí too much, and the church felt like his assassin.

I reluctantly headed towards his culminating work. I was lost in my thoughts and looking at the ground. However, when I turned a corner and looked up, I was awestruck by his creation.

"Gio!" My friend's voice released me from my trance. Samuru had been working as a stone cutter and assistant architect for decades, and we had been friends since he visited my area five or six years ago. Although he had invited me to see him at his workshop at Sagrada Familia several times, this was the first time I accepted. We embraced warmly, and then Samuru motioned for me to follow him.

He led me to a bench from which we had a complete view of the church. As soon as we sat down, he pulled out some lunches he had picked up earlier. "Always the planner!" I said jokingly. "You. Rarely the planner!" he replied without skipping a beat.

I opened my lunch box because I was famished. Inside it, I found a small omelet, two chicken skewers, three slices of fantastic bread, some fruit and cheese, and a small flask of wine.

"How are you, my friend?" I asked as I stuffed half the omelet into my mouth. Samuru laughed. "Let's eat first; I only had coffee this morning." So we ate our food before catching up on our friendship.

I mixed the wine with sparkling water, and after taking a few gulps, I finally spoke. "How are you, my friend?" I asked. Samuru put his finger up to wait, put a piece of cheese in his mouth, gulped some wine, and then answered, "Fine." We laughed.

"Gio, have you seen that photo of Gaudí with his head shaved?" I nodded, knowing what he was about to say. "Has anyone ever told you that you look a lot like him in that photo?" I rolled my eyes. "Yes," I said.

We were relaxing on the bench, admiring Sagrada Familia, when my friend turned to me and asked, "What do you feel and see, Gio?"

"I feel amazed," I began, "the building looks like a living organism, almost as if it is alive and the workers on the scaffolding are watering it. The colors, symbols of nature, curves, and shapes of the building suggest life - something growing, breathing, and alive. This is what I can see. What about you?"

I was surprised when I saw tears welling up in Samuru's eyes in response to my question.

"When I started working here," he began, "I was primarily focused on learning new designing techniques. It was all about adding to my portfolio of design and stonework that was driving me. But the more time I spent here, the more my focus changed. I changed, too. Did you know that I converted my religion from Buddhist to Catholic?" I must have looked shocked because Samuru added, "Yes, Gio, now we share the same religion, but I don't think you practice yours much?" I opened my mouth to respond but just got the word "But..." out before he continued. "I realized that I couldn't learn by just looking at Gaudí; I had to look at what Gaudí was looking at. So here we are, looking at what Gaudí was looking at. The church is just a symbol, or many symbols, for what lies beyond and in this man's heart. Isn't it amazing, Gio?" he asked.

I turned and looked again. What had seemed an incredible arrangement of stone and tile now looked different. It was more than its parts, and my friend began unveiling it for me.

"Come," said Samuru as he got up, gesturing for me to follow him towards the church. "Gaudí only managed to complete one section of the facade during his lifetime. He struggled to finish it because he believed that if anyone saw this completed part, they would be convinced that the rest of the building had to be completed. He was so sure about the message of this facade section that he risked his reputation on it. It faces east, from where the sun, the source of life, rises. Now stand next to me and tell me what you see."

I stopped to take it all in but it was overwhelming. "What's your first impression?" my friend asked. "It's like stalactites growing in caves. It looks like a natural stone formation. But then I see people, plants, and animals intertwining, telling a story."

Samuru nodded and said, "It's all a story, but I find it fascinating. Can you see the doors below, Gio?" I nodded. "The one on the left is called 'Hope,' the one on the right is dedicated to 'Faith,' and the central one is called 'Love.' Can you understand why?'"

There were so many figures that my mind was getting confused. Samuru noticed my confusion and offered a suggestion. "Start from the middle," he said.

"Isn't this the birth of Christ?" I asked. "Yes, actually," Samuru replied. "This whole side of the church is called the Nativity Facade. Looking at the most important story above the central door, you will see other stories leading up to it and flowing from it. Focus only on the human figures for now," he suggested.

As I looked at the scene while listening to Samuru, it started to make sense. My friend pointed and said, "The figure on the left is Joseph; he only had a promise to go on." I tried to remember the story of Joseph, who was married to Mary. Seeing my expression, Samuru gave me more hints, "Joseph had planned out his future, but then he had a dream that changed everything. He had to take this woman and her child, who was not his own, and trust in something greater than himself. He only had his dreams to hold onto and hoped his path would be revealed. Hope is something you want but don't yet possess. So Joseph becomes the personification of hope because he only had words to believe in, a dream to cling to, but he hoped they would be fulfilled."

My friend then asked me to focus on what I saw on the right.

"This part is called faith, and the dominant figure is Mary. She appears in all the scenes," Samuru said, pointing. So faith is..." he paused to let me finish the sentence. I must have picked up on his thought because I said: "So faith is when someone believes what they don't see because they've seen something. For example, when I see a part but not the whole, I see something so beautiful that I believe something must be behind it. Or I meet someone who has a presence that I can't define. "Yes, Yes," Samura added and continued, " Mary saw the angel and maybe didn't understand what would unfold in her life, but she said, 'Yes.' She trusted what she saw and heard. Does that make sense, Gio?" I nodded as I gazed at the stone, which had taken on a life of its own.

We then moved to the center, where Samuru began by saying, "This part is called love and is dedicated to Christ." He then motioned for me to look at the carved figures and describe their meaning. Although I could see the figures, I couldn't understand how they came together. Samuru allowed me to reflect for a few minutes, and then he said, "Love is when I am embraced by the one I hoped for and believed. Love is when the space in the heart finds that it is full."

I looked from side to side. "It's like hope is the desire, faith is the road, and love is the arrival." "Gio! I didn't know you were a theologian!" Samuru said, chuckling.

We then changed positions, and Samuru pointed upwards, continuing the conversation.

"I want you to look at two more things before we enter. First, examine the faces of the figures. Pay attention to the three magi, the shepherds, Joseph, and Mary. What do you notice?" I looked at each figure carefully, taking note of their expressions. "I can see that some look surprised, some are fascinated, and everyone seems to be at peace." "Exactly," my friend replied.

He continued, "The second thing I want you to observe is nature. Look at the trees, plants, animals, and insects. Gaudí intentionally included each element and each carries a precise meaning. However, for you, what does it all represent?"

A great tree above us looked like the tree of life. On the sides were columns held up by a turtle and a tortoise. The tree was populated with birds that resembled turkeys or ducks, crawling insects, a snake biting an apple, snails, and even a chameleon. After admiring the tree, I finally replied, "Somehow, nature and these human stories are intertwined." "Yes, my friend," said Samuru, "For Gaudí, there is no contradiction between the story of creation and redemption. He believed that nature was the greatest homage to God, so he copied it instead of trying to change it. All of this, the plants, the animals, and the joyful stories about the nativity are like a hymn. It is a song written in stone. Gaudí hoped those who saw it would perceive this and want the hymn to continue and grow even after he was gone."

I was so engrossed in my thoughts that I didn't hear Samuru calling me. He pulled my arm and asked, "Gio, do you want to see inside now?" I nodded while looking up.

"There is one condition, Gio," he said. I looked at him, puzzled. "You have to follow me in while looking down at the floor. Do not look up until I tell you. Can you do that?" I laughed, but he was serious.

"Yes," I agreed and followed him through the main door.

"Okay, Gio, you can look up now."

"Holy fuck!" I exclaimed. Towering above us was a forest made of stone and glass and light. I turned in circles and kept repeating, "Holy fuck!" until Samuru squeezed my arm and put his finger to his lips.

I felt tears welling up, and my voice cracked when I asked Samuru, "What is this place?"

He replied, "This is Gaudí's soul."

We were surrounded by a radiant light emanating from all directions. Samuru allowed me to take it all in before continuing, "Other architects have copied each other throughout history, but Gaudí copied nature. He believed there was no greater tribute to the Creator than to replicate His creation, and that's exactly what he did here."

I was overwhelmed. It was as if I was a tiny ant standing amidst boundless beauty.

"You are looking at thirty-six columns holding up the structure," Samuru whispered. "Each column represents a different person in history. As you can see, the symbols on each column honor these individuals. For example, Mathew is represented by one column, Mark by another, Luke by a third, and John by the fourth. These are the writers of the four gospels," he explained, pointing at each one.

"The windows of this church are also symbolic. If you look at the nativity side, you will notice that the colors of the glass are yellow, green, and blue. These colors are meant to represent promise and hope and have a calming effect. Now, if you look at the passion side of the church, which represents challenges and suffering, you will see that the colors are different. Here, we have yellow, orange, and red - the color of blood. However, these colors also represent passion. Gaudí was a passionate man, and this is an aspect that few biographers have written about."

"The colors on the windows change from dark to light, lifting your eyes as you look at them. This is not by accident. We start with red, representing our connection to the earth, then move up to orange, and finally to yellow, representing glory. These colors invite us to begin with passion, move through acceptance, and end with love. They also represent a journey from suffering to healing to fulfillment, which hints at the resurrection."

Samuru's voice was like the background music to what my eyes were trying to take in. It was almost overwhelming. "Can we sit down?" I asked. "Gio, are you alright?" he asked as we sat.

Without knowing why, I started crying like a baby. It was just too much. I put my finger up for him to give me a minute. Once I pulled myself together, I found myself gazing towards the altar.

When he saw where I was looking, Samuru asked, "What do you think of the Baldacchino?" I chuckled. "It sort of looks like an umbrella," I said while wiping my eyes. "But look closer, Gio," he urged me. As I observed, I noticed the hanging lamps with decorative symbols of nature, such as grapes and leaves. A crucifix was also hanging below it, and words and letters were written on all sides. "What does it mean?" I asked.

"Everything in Gaudí's life has to be taken in the correct context. Now, look above the vault and tell me what you see?"

"It looks like a triangle within a circle," I replied.

"Exactly! So, there is the representation of the Father. Now, look at the canopy. The lamps almost look like flames, like tongues of fire, representing the Holy Spirit. The writing around the sides is the seven gifts of the Holy Spirit: wisdom, understanding, counsel, fortitude, knowledge, piety, and fear of the Lord. Now, below, you see the crucifix. So, there you have it: the center of the church is also the center of this faith - the Father, Son, and Holy Spirit, the Trinity. That is what it means."

We stood up from our seats and turned to take in the view once more. Then, I turned to Samuru and asked, "This is amazing, but can you tell me more about Gaudí as a person?" Samuru replied, "Look around you; everything you see here reflects who he was." I objected, "But what about the stories that portray him as someone who let himself go? Stories about him being homeless, that he never showered, and he wore rags. He seems like a bit of a loser," I said without thinking. "Sorry," I added.

Samuru didn't react; he just looked up and around before turning to face me.

"First of all, many of those stories are exaggerated. There is a story that Gaudí held his underwear together with safety pins. I laughed when I read that one. I don't believe that, so you must take some of this as hearsay. These stories are born from people's attempts to fill in the missing gaps and reduce Gaudí to something they can understand, like a homeless man. However, one thing is true: Gaudí was not interested in the material things that fill our lives. He was a man in evolution, and though he initially wanted to make his mark and find success and wealth, he eventually lost interest in fame, wealth, popularity, and social status. It was as if he was destined for something greater. If you want to understand who Gaudí was, don't focus on his clothes, housing, or anything that preoccupies our minds. Instead, go to Sagrada Familia and look up. There, you can glimpse what Gaudí's horizon was and where his true interests lay.

As we left, my friend Samuru said, "I came here to transform stone, and I found that the stone has transformed me."

I traveled to Barcelona to discover Gaudí, and I left changed by him.

# Chapter 8
# Almost

I'm a solo sailor, and I know how risky it can be. To avoid any mishaps, I always take precautions. But this one time, I decided to take a chance.

When you're sailing alone, it's crucial that someone on land knows your itinerary and route details. My friend Matteo played this role for me and still does.I remember chatting with Matteo a few days before I set sail in September. We went over my route and checked the weather forecast. I planned to leave from Brindisi, stop in Sicily, and finally reach Tunis. The route was longer and more challenging than usual, but I had enough experience to handle it.

Matteo advised against it, though. "Don't go," he said. "The weather is unpredictable. Wait a week to see." His words still echo in my head.

Weather forecasts are always estimates based on collected data from the past and currents from the present. Together, the data gives a reasonably good prediction of what to expect, but it is always an educated guess since the weather is fluid. According to the forecasts, the upcoming sail looked fair, with a possible risk of strong winds and storms. However, I had sailed into worse forecasts before, so I didn't see any reason to postpone. September was already pushing it, so I thanked my friend for his concern, established our days and modes of check-ins, and planned to set off.

I have an engine on my sailboat, but because of limited fuel, I only use it in an emergency or if I get stuck. Since I was going on a longer sail, I filled and checked the engine, replenished supplies, and reviewed every inch of my sails and rigging to ensure everything was in good condition.

I set off from Brindisi one Thursday morning at sunrise. I've sailed the Ionian Sea many times before, so I was sure I could do it with my eyes closed, regardless of the weather. I dropped a message to Matteo saying, "Day one, all clear." I decided to take my time and enjoy the trip, so I stuck close to the coast of Sicily. I passed Taormina, which looked amazing from the water, Catania, which brought back some bad memories, and Syracuse, my favorite Sicilian town. I docked my boat in Syracuse and secured it.

I wandered through the town's white stone streets and ended up in the main square, where I saw Athena's 5th-century BC temple, now the town's cathedral. I grabbed a meal in the piazza and then went inside the church. I sat in the cool, dark space, feeling peaceful. "Hi God, it's Gio," I said.

After a few moments, I returned to the marina and sat on my deck, watching the setting sun transform the water into fiery lapping tongues. "Beautiful," I said out loud.

I fell asleep and then woke up abruptly a few hours later to the swaying of the boat as the waves had grown stronger and the wind had picked up. I checked the boat's rigging and saw no issues, so I went back to sleep.

The following day, I woke up early and put the coffee on. While it was brewing, I checked the latest weather report as I needed to sail towards Tunis and pass Malta. Possible storms were predicted, but I didn't want to stop in Malta because it would prolong my trip.

I sent Matteo a message saying, "All clear; heading further into the Mediterranean today." Despite the wind and waves picking up, I was well within my safety range and felt confident that I would soon be relaxing at the Sidi Bou Said marina, about twenty miles from Tunis. Once there, I looked forward to exploring the Medina and visiting the Roman-era mosaics in the Bardo Museum. After that, I had planned to spend five or six days at Hammamet Beach, where I would find crystal clear waters, powdery sand, and excellent snorkeling.

The waters were calm as I left Sicily and sailed past Malta. However, as predicted by the forecast, the winds began to pick up, and I had to keep a close eye on the rigging and steer the boat in the right direction.

Unfortunately, when I was halfway towards Pantelleria, the weather suddenly worsened. At first,

I assumed it was just heavy rain, but then all hell broke loose, and I found myself in the middle of a severe storm.

I had heard of Mendicanes, which are tropical-like cyclones that can occur in the Mediterranean Sea, but I had never experienced one. As the waves began tossing the ship and the winds intensified, I had to furl the sail and secure the rigging to prevent damage. The boat was bobbing up and down, tossed by waves that started to reach ten, then fifteen feet, and more. Steering was impossible, so I tried to clear the storm using the engine.

Hours passed as I struggled to maneuver out, but the storm surrounded me. I turned off the motor to conserve fuel to wait it out. I told myself that my boat was strong and that I had enough experience to get through this.

As the night approached, the winds continued to gust, and the waves grew even higher, making it almost impossible to navigate the boat. I felt like a toy being tossed around by a giant. To add to my troubles, the boxes of supplies on the deck were sliding around. I needed to secure them without getting thrown into the water. I grabbed a rope, tied it around my waist, climbed the ladder to the deck, and secured the other end to the mast, leaving enough slack to secure the supplies.

I collected some of the boxes and placed them on the landing below. I had three more to move when a massive wave hit the boat. The sudden impact lifted the boat at least 20 feet and then dropped it. This strong jolt threw me in the air, tightening my rope. Then the rope snapped, and I was thrown into the air. On the way down, I hit my arm against the boat's edge and fell overboard into the water.

As I spat out seawater and tried to regain my bearings, I told myself, "Gio, you got this."

Though I didn't panic, I knew I was in trouble unless I managed to get back on board. My left arm throbbed with pain, saltwater splashed into my eyes and mouth, and darkness surrounded me.

I was completely alone out here. It was just me and the boat, and I needed to get back onboard.

My security system was the EPIRB (Emergency Position Indicator Radio Beacon), which is mounted to my boat and requires an operator to turn it on. I hadn't activated it before going overboard, so no one would know I was in trouble.

I struggled to get back on the boat, but the waves were so high they kept pushing me away.

Suddenly, a massive wave hit me, submerging me and flipping me upside down. Disoriented, I held my breath and tried to stay calm, hoping to float towards the surface.

I wondered if this was the end. Had all my life experiences led me to this point, only to be washed away at sea? Was this the death that my chosen path had in store for me? At thirty-seven, I didn't feel ready to die, as I was only beginning to understand life. Would I have to leave behind lessons half-learned and hopes unfulfilled?

I suddenly emerged from the water, gasping for air and spitting out seawater. It took me a few minutes to catch my breath.

"Think, Gio!" I shouted to myself. I knew I couldn't count on being rescued by a passing boat or the Coast Guard, as the wind and waves were too high for me to be seen.

I spotted my boat, and the distance was becoming insurmountable. I tried to paddle with one arm but made no progress.

For the second time in twenty-four hours, I prayed. "God, this is Gio. I need your help."

With renewed determination, I used every ounce of my strength to kick towards the boat. I used both legs and swam with one arm, fighting against the waves, wind, and rain.

Despite hours of effort, I had only managed to get about ten feet closer to the boat. But I didn't give up because ten feet was still progress.

My left arm was throbbing, and I was sure that I had broken it. I relied on my right arm to keep my head up while I kicked with my legs. I kept spitting out water and tried to keep my eyes on the bobbing boat through the rain. "Gio, you can do this," I repeated to myself.

After paddling for another half an hour, the storm started to calm down. The wind and waves became more manageable, which helped me make better progress. I padded and kicked with all my might for what seemed like hours.

Although my left arm was numb, I used my right arm and legs to inch myself closer to the boat, now only about thirty feet away.

"Damn, how am I going to get on board?" I asked myself. I have a removable boarding ladder onboard, but I had it stored below deck since I only deployed it in calm weather for swimming—my mistake.

With one able arm, I couldn't climb up the side without the ladder. But as I inched closer, I saw a way. The snapped rope was dangling over the edge, and if I could tie it around my waist, I could use my legs to climb up the side. Once I reached the top, I could grab onto something with my good arm and flip myself into the boat.

The storm was calming down, but I wasn't sure if it was over. I was in the water next to the boat, bobbing up and down and splashing water all around me. I tried to grab the end of the rope hanging off the side of the boat, but I quickly realized that it wasn't long enough to tie it around my waist while I was still in the water.

"Think, Gio," I told myself.

I reached down and realized the rope had snapped in two, leaving a double length still around my waist. As I considered my options, an idea began to form in my mind.

To get onto the side of the boat, I had to unwind one length of the rope from my waist, tie it to the other end, and pull myself up. It seemed pretty straightforward, except for my arm.

# A Life on a Sailboat

There was no other way, so I paddled under the rope and searched for a small ledge on the side where I could put one foot. I was grateful that the wind and waves had died down considerably, but it was still raining hard, making it difficult to see.

I grabbed the hanging rope and positioned myself below the support of the boarding ladder, where two small ladder supports protruded.

My plan was to hold the dangling rope so that I could stand on the two ladder supports; from that position, I could tie the rope around my waist to the one dangling from the boat. Then, I would brace my feet against the boat and attempt to walk up the side horizontally, looping the rope around my arm as I climbed up.

I wrapped the rope from the boat around my right arm and tried to pull myself up, but I didn't have enough leverage. My feet kept slipping on the side of the boat. I realized that I needed my other arm to climb. I grabbed the rope with my left arm and used it to hold my position as I climbed with my right arm. Despite the excruciating pain that shot through my body, I refused to let go. I used my left arm to stabilize myself and reached up with my right arm until I could place one foot on the support. The pain was unbearable, but I persisted and managed to get into a horizontal position. Then, I pulled myself up to get my other foot on the support.

I focused all my strength on my right arm to lift myself and stabilize my left foot on the ledge. I don't know how I managed it, but I did. Then, I used my teeth to grab and pull some slack from the rope wrapped around my arm. I needed my left arm to tie the two ropes together, but the pain was unbearable, and my fingers were numb. However, I didn't see any other way to do it. With my feet on the supports and the rope around my right arm, I had to tie it to the rope around my waist to climb up the remaining distance.

This situation could go either way, but I figured it was better to lose an arm than my life. I used my numb fingers to tie the two ends together; somehow, I tied one, two, and three knots. I now had the leverage I needed.

I braced my feet against the boat and let myself go horizontally, hoping the rope would hold. Using the taught rope, I took one step after another, slowly walking up the side. The ladder area of the boat was rough, providing enough friction for me to prevent slipping. With every inch, the strain became unbearable. One inch, two inches, three inches. "Fuck, Gio, don't give up!" I shouted.

As I neared the top, a massive wave suddenly lifted the boat. The force was so strong that it threw me up in the air, and I landed on the deck on my injured arm.

I cursed in pain and dragged myself to the cabin. There, I quickly activated my emergency indicator beacon (EPIRB) and then fell unconscious.

I remember being surrounded by blue and red lights and men speaking Italian. One said, "It's badly broken; we have to airlift him...". I moaned, "My boat, my boat." Another man patted my head and said, "Don't worry; we have your boat; we will tow it. We are going to take care of you. You're safe."

I have some disconnected memories of a helicopter, an ambulance, a stretcher, doctors, and surgical masks. Somewhere along the way, I heard Matteo's voice.

It was daylight when I started to open my eyes. I could see five people at the foot of my bed; one seemed to be a doctor, and the other four, I couldn't make out. Then I heard Matteo's voice. "He is awake! Gio, it's Matteo, your brother!" I blinked to try to focus. I couldn't turn or sit up since my left arm was in a cast with dozens of pins sticking out. "Gio!" a female voice said. "It's Masika, and Sadiki is here too." "I am here too, Gio!" added Chiara, Matteo's wife. As I looked at my friends, tears streamed down my face. "Awww, we're here to make you happy, not make you cry!" Masika said, kissing me on the forehead.

It was difficult for me to speak, but in between sobs, I managed to say, "I thought I had lost you."

"Never," Matteo replied, "Never, never, never," he said, squeezing my hand.

I looked around and asked, "Where am I?" Sadiki answered, "You're in the hospital in Catania. I'm so glad we were in Brindisi when Matteo called us. We flew down here this morning." "But..." I started to say; Matteo anticipated my thoughts. "Don't worry about your boat; it's in Catania. You can't sail it to Brindisi; my friend, that was a bad fracture. The doctor said that staying out there for a few more hours would have cost you not only your arm but also your life. They had to put you back together. I'll take care of the boat, Gio. Our wives gave Sadiki and me permission to sail to Brindisi, where you can organize repairs. But for now, your only concern is to heal."

I must have fallen asleep because when I woke up, the sun was setting, and Sadiki and Masika were sitting by my bedside. "Gio, can you hear me?" Masika asked. I nodded in response. "Matteo and Chiara have gone to check on your boat and to find lodging. The doctor wants you to stay here for at least a week before returning to Brindisi. We'll stay with you and bring you home. Chiara and I will fly with you while Matteo and Sadiki sail your boat. I wanted to tell you this so that you don't worry."

I don't know if it was the painkillers, but I felt emotional. Tears rolled down my face again as Sadiki caressed my head and said, "Awww, Gio, we are so happy to be with you. You're family." I looked at these two people, whose lives had intersected with mine, and felt an overwhelming sense of gratitude and affection.

We eventually did make it back to Brindisi, but I had to stay in the hospital longer because the doctor had to reset some of the pins. It took several months for my arm to heal, and even today, during the winter months, I feel a deep ache where the bone was fractured.

I am grateful for that ache because it reminds me of what I almost lost that day and makes me appreciate what I have been given.

# Chapter 9
# Mystery in Mykonos

Mykonos had been calling me for a few years, and I couldn't resist its lure forever. I knew the island was known as a gay mecca, party central, and destination for college-age crowds. But I was curious to explore other aspects of the island and wondered if it had more to offer beyond glitter and beer.

I arrived at Tourlos Marina on a Thursday morning, and I chose it because it offered safe docking, showers, a supermarket, and complete services for my vessel. It was an ideal location, only a twenty-minute walk from Mykonos town.

I was excited to begin my exploration, so I quickly showered, put on shorts and sandals, and headed out. As I approached the town, I was amazed by its beauty. I had expected it to be touristy and tacky, but instead, I was surrounded by whitewashed buildings that framed a picturesque beach. The shops and houses along the winding stone streets were taken straight out of a storybook.

Few people were out and about, so I decided to sit for a morning coffee at a waterfront café and take in the view.

After a few minutes, I noticed around a dozen small paintings of ships on water lined up against the curb in front of the cafe. The images were simple, in the style of a 6th grader, but the colors were bright, and there was something happy about them.

I sat down and ordered a coffee, gradually becoming aware of my surroundings. Sitting behind me was a middle-aged woman looking at her phone; she had a few of the same small paintings on her table, so I assumed she was the artist.

After taking a few sips of coffee, I introduced myself. "Hi, my name is Jovanny, and I really like your art. Do you live in Mykonos?" It took her a moment to realize I was speaking to her, but then she turned and smiled. "You may need another coffee too!" I joked, motioning for the waiter to bring us two more.

"Thank you for asking," she replied. "Yes, I do live here. My name is Elizabeth, and I've been in Mykonos for almost ten years." I was curious. "Wow, that's impressive. How did you manage to make a life for yourself here?"

As our second cup of coffee arrived, hot and delicious, my brain cells slowly woke up.

"I'd been thinking about living in Mykonos for almost a decade before I finally made the move," she said. "The problem was always the money. My pension, savings, and social security wouldn't cut it on the island. But I was determined to make my dream a reality. So, I flew to Mykonos for a few weeks to check things out. During my visit, I looked into the costs of renting a place away from the touristy spots, utilities, food, and other living expenses. After a lot of research, I worked out the monthly amount I needed to live in Mykonos."

I nodded and listened, intrigued.

"I used to have a boring office job, but it had good benefits and a small pension plan. Outside of work, I always found solace in art. Even as a child, art was my go-to for getting creative. I would draw, paint, or design images when I wasn't at school or, as an adult, working. However, I wasn't thinking about art while on that investigative trip. I realized that I needed more money every month than I would have after retirement, but I couldn't see how. I came home with a clearer idea of what it would take to live in Mykonos, but I also felt sad because it didn't seem possible unless I won the lottery." She laughed.

"After my two-week vacation, I returned to my daily routine. One evening, while I was working on a painting of a beach in Mykonos based on a photo I had taken, a friend dropped by, and I shared my story with her. Out of the blue, she said, 'Why not sell your artwork in Mykonos? You have talent; why not use it to realize your dream?' At first, I thought this was ridiculous; I told myself I wasn't good enough and my art wasn't good enough. But every day, I kept thinking about it, and every time I picked up my brush, I asked myself, 'Why not?'"

"Now, don't get me wrong," Elizabeth continued. "I realized that I would be rolling the dice. What if nobody bought my art? What if I couldn't make it work? What if I lost everything? What if I had to return to the United States and admit I had made a huge mistake? What if, what if, what if…"

"I grew tired of the 'what ifs.' A year before my retirement, I realized that unless I took a chance, I would be stuck in a life that I didn't want. So, a week after my retirement, I gave up my apartment, got rid of my belongings, packed two suitcases with clothes and art supplies, flew to Athens, and came to Mykonos. I've been here ever since."

"I'm so impressed," I exclaimed. "How are your art sales going?"

Elizabeth beamed, "Better than I could have hoped for. Last week, I sold a large piece to an American celebrity, and my work is gaining popularity both on and off the island. Typically, I sell around a dozen of these smaller paintings each day, which more than covers my expenses. Whenever I get a commission for a bigger painting, it's just the icing on the cake. I can use that extra cash to explore new places I've never been."

I reached for my wallet, hoping to purchase one of her small paintings as a token of her bravery. Although she offered me one for free, I politely declined, knowing she relied on the sales. I chose my favorite painting, gave her some euros, and expressed gratitude for sharing her story.

# Onward

After we went our separate ways, meeting her made my horizons feel even broader.

As I approached the town center, I noticed a pelican strolling down the street. I wondered if it was the famous mascot and greeted the bird before continuing my exploration. As I looked around, I noticed that all the shops were deserted. "Where is everybody?" I wondered. It was then that I realized that they were probably at the beach.

I left the shopping area and hitched a ride to Super Paradise Beach.

As a 37-year-old, I didn't want to feel out of place among the crowds of young people. However, I felt my age as I walked through the bar area and past the DJ blasting music. I stepped onto the sand and saw hundreds of twenty-somethings frolicking around. But then, I caught sight of the crystal blue waves of the water, which were calling out. "Yes," I said, looking for a spot on the beach.

I needed to find someone to watch my things while I went for a swim. Most of my valuables were safe at the marina, but I still had my wallet with cash and driver's license. I stripped down to my bathing suit and walked along the sand, searching for someone trustworthy. Finding someone responsible among the sea of drunken college-age students was difficult. But then, I saw two men sunbathing under an oversized umbrella, surrounded by beach gear, and about my same age.

I immediately knew they were gay. They had toned bodies and wore speedos, designer sunglasses, and had matching tattoos. I asked, "Do you speak English?" and one of them responded, "A little." I asked if they were Italian, and they said, "Si, si! From Rome!" When I shared that I was from Brindisi, one of them jumped up and high-fived me. "I have to ask a favor," I continued, "I want to go in the water, but I'm afraid to leave my things on the beach. Could I..." One of them, Roberto, interrupted me and said, "Sure, you can leave your things here. You can have this spot next to us as your base. We'll stay here when you're in the water, and you can watch our things when we go in." We struck a deal.

I threw down my sunglasses and hat, tossed my sandals aside, and ran across the sand. Without hesitation, I dove in head-first.

I feel a bond with the sea; in her waters, I feel peace on the inside, and on the outside, I feel connected.

The water was warm, clear, and glorious.

I swam away from the noisy crowd and stayed far from the shore to avoid the party scene. After almost an hour, I returned to the beach to give my friends a chance to swim.

"By the way," I said, feeling awkward, "my name is Jovanny, but my friends call me Gio." I had forgotten to introduce myself earlier.

Roberto responded, "Io mi chiamo Roberto, e mio compagno e' Martino - My name is Roberto and my partner is Martino."

# Onward

I sat down to soak up the sun. "If you'd like to share the umbrella, you're welcome to," Martino offered. I thanked them and laid back. "I'll just stay in the sun for a few minutes," I said before drifting off to sleep.

Upon waking up, Roberto and Martino kindly offered me a bottle of cold water. I moved under their umbrella to escape the intense sun. "Jovanny," Martino asked, "what brings you here? And how is it that you live in Brindisi? And are you gay?" Roberto glanced at Martino, then turned to me, and we all laughed.

I figured I would start by letting them know who I was. "I'm not gay. But..." I trailed off and stopped myself before I almost said that I had friends who were gay, so I don't have a problem with that. I realized how dumb that would sound. I noticed the two looking at me as these thoughts crossed my mind, so I continued: "It's so great to meet you guys!" They both nodded. I told them about my life, sailing adventures, and why I came to Mykonos. "Why don't you take it easy here this afternoon, and later on, we can show you around Mykonos town?" I smiled and nodded. Martino indicated he was ready for a swim, so he got up while Roberto volunteered to look after our belongings.

"Jovanny, how far out can you swim?" Martino shouted. "As far out as you can, times two," I responded. A bit of competition started, but I let Martino go beyond me since I didn't know the currents. "I thought you could swim further?" he taunted me. "I can, but I don't want to," I replied. Martino laughed and then swam towards me as we both tread water.

I asked, "You and Roberto seem like a cool couple. How long have you been together?" "Five years now," he replied. "It seems like yesterday. We're good together. I'm so happy I met him," he continued. Then Martino asked, "How long have you been...single?" I laughed and said, "Sometimes I think my boat is my wife! She is demanding, does not want to be left alone, and always gets back at me if I neglect her." Martino found this funny and asked, "Maybe you should try a man?" I laughed and replied, "My boat is a jealous lover; she would neither tolerate man nor woman. But, Martino, do you ever long to be with a woman?" His face took on the expression of someone who just bit into a lemon, and he shook his head emphatically. "I feel the same about being with a man," I said. He laughed.

After a brief silence, Martino asked me, "Are you searching for a woman on Mykonos?" I wasn't sure if I had any particular goal for my visit to the island, so I shook my head. "No, I don't think so. I came to Mykonos for the island and am open to whatever might come my way. Maybe I'll make new friends." Martino responded, "That would be a wonderful gift." We then swam back to shore.

When we returned to our umbrella, Roberto had already prepared three cold beers and a tray of snacks. "You guys are too much!" I exclaimed in English, but neither understood what I said, and I didn't know how to translate it into Italian. So the three of us sat in the shade, sipping our beers, munching on chips, nibbling on sliced cheese and salami, and watching the other sunbathers.

"Jovanny," Roberto began, "which of these ladies is your type? I can introduce you to her. Just let me know which one". I looked at him and then at Martino, wondering if they were serious. "Are you saying that if I tell you which women here I'm interested in, you'll go over and introduce me to them?" I asked. Roberto nodded. "You're a handsome man, Jovanny. Any gay man would love to be with you, so I think women would be the same. So, which one?" I laughed at the seriousness in his voice. "You must be joking. I'm not telling you which one is my type". They both tried to get more information from me, but I didn't give them any hints. Finding a girl for Jovanny became a running joke for them.

Hours passed, and the sun was starting to set. 'Why don't you two go in for a last swim while I watch our things?' I suggested. Roberto and Martino looked at each other, nodded, and ran to the water. I sat on one of the lounges and watched the people stroll by. As they passed, a few men looked in my direction, but none of the women. I guess they thought I was gay. "Their loss," I sighed, putting a newspaper over my face.

The next thing I knew, Roberto was shaking me. "Wake up, Jovanny! You're going to sleep all night!" he said, laughing. "We will drive you back to town.

Then we can meet for dinner. Is that OK with you?" Roberto asked. He had been speaking in Italian before but had now switched to somewhat smooth English. I was half asleep when I got up and started gathering my things. "Poor Jovanny, so tired. You sit here while we pack up." I did as suggested and gradually came to my senses. In a few minutes, we were trudging across the sand towards the car.

As we walked, the conversation switched back to Italian. Roberto asked, "Jovanny, take a look at Martino. Do you think he has a muscular body?" I looked at him and said, "Huh?" Roberto continued, "Martino always says he has a bad body, no muscles, is ugly, and so on. What do you think? I want to ask you an honest opinion from a straight man." I looked at Martino and replied, "He is the most muscular man on the beach... well, next to me, of course." They laughed. "But seriously, all that negativity is just in his head. Nobody sees Martino as a small, skinny, or ugly man. And if you don't believe me, didn't you see the women looking at both of you when you were walking towards the water? That's why they were ignoring me!" They laughed again.

"Martino," I said, putting my arm on his shoulder, "you have these thoughts because you don't think you're good enough. You are! Meeting you and Roberto has been a beautiful experience for me, and both of you are beautiful, inside and out." There was a pause, and Roberto broke the silence as we walked. "Meeting you, Jovanny, has been an unexpected gift. Thank you for hanging out with two gay boys!" We then piled into their tiny car.

We spoke little since we were sleepy from laying in the sun most of the day. "There's a great seafood place in town that I think you'll enjoy. Later on, we can explore the nightlife," Roberto suggested.

It took us only a few minutes to reach the marina, where I went straight to my boat and dozed off until Roberto called out to me. "Damn, is it 8:30 already?" I asked as I climbed up the ladder onto the deck. Roberto shook his head. "Give me ten minutes for a shower," I said, grabbing a towel and soap before heading to the marina showers.

"I'm Sorry," I said as I hopped into their car. "We're Italians; we're used to being late," Roberto said cheerfully.

We then drove off, breaking all speed limits, and arrived at our destination right on time.

The men did a fantastic job of finding a beautiful restaurant on a hilltop with a breathtaking view. From there, we could see the beach and the illuminated town below.

Given that every other restaurant was packed, I was curious to know how they managed to find such a fantastic place. Before I could ask, Martino placed his hand on my arm and gestured towards Roberto. "He has connections," he said with a nod, leaving me thoroughly impressed.

I knew my seafood like others knew their wines, so when the waiter came to our table, I asked if I could see the fish before ordering. Without batting an eye, he motioned for us to follow him. Upon entering the kitchen area, I immediately noticed the absence of a strong fish odor, which was a good sign.

I asked the waiter, "Which fish are fresh and local?" He smiled, seemingly pleased that I was knowledgeable, and responded, "The rule of thumb is that the larger fish are imported but never frozen, while the smaller ones are local. To be more precise..." He walked down the row of fish on ice and pointed out, "local, not local, local, local, local, imported…."

One fish in particular caught my attention. "And what about this one, the Lavraki; how fresh is it, and is it local or not?" The waiter nodded, impressed. "You have a good eye. The Lavraki, also known as the Sea Bass, is fresh and local and was caught this morning." But then I threw him a curveball. "Is it wild-caught or farm-raised?" The waiter looked shocked. "My good man!" he said. "You ask the right questions, and it is a pleasure to work with you. Other restaurants may serve farm-raised Lavraki, which is often cheaper. However, our seafood, including our Lavraki, is 100% wild-caught, and if you order this fish, you will see that it will melt in your mouth and is delicious grilled without many seasonings." I looked at my friends, who nodded in agreement. "Three Lavraki dinners, please, and the sides will be the chef's choice." The waiter bowed, and we returned to our table.

# Onward

Roberto looked at me curiously and asked, "Jovanny, how did you know to ask those questions?" The waiter arrived with a bottle of wine, interrupting him. "The chef recommends this wine to go with your fish," he said. When we hesitated, he added, "It's not expensive, but it's perfect with grilled Lavraki." It was as if he had read our minds. The waiter poured a bit into Martino's glass, who took a sip, smiled, and nodded his approval.

"To answer your question, Roberto," I began, "I've been living on a sailboat since I was 22, and now I'm 37. I rely on food from the sea, and I've been to so many ports that I can tell good seafood from bad a mile away. I don't want to waste my time or money on bad food, so I've learned to ask questions. You'll see; I can almost taste the Lavraki now, and I believe it'll be just as the waiter described." As we sipped our chilled, dry white wine, the waiter arrived with unsolicited seafood appetizers sent by the chef.

The Lavraki was grilled to perfection, with a delicate and flaky texture. The side dishes of white rice and a cucumber, tomato, and olive salad were simple, allowing the flavors to shine. The waiter approached us with a smile, checking to see if everything was OK. We nodded, and he left after refilling our wine glasses. He discreetly placed another unsolicited bottle on our table.

Roberto said, "There are certain moments in life that you never forget, and this is one of them. Thank you, Jovanny," he lifted his glass for a toast. "To friendship," he added, and we all repeated. As I looked at Roberto and Martin, their bond, love, and affection were almost glowing; I almost wished for something, but I didn't know what.

I felt grateful to have met these two; in just eight hours, it felt like we had lived a lifetime together.

"Jovanny, please be careful of your drinking. We have the whole evening ahead of us," Roberto reminded me as I poured myself another glass. I looked at him quizzically. "We want to explore Mykonos at night with you after dinner. It's a must-see, Jovanny! You may even find the woman of your dreams!" he chuckled. "I don't need you to set me up, my friend, but we can definitely go out and explore. But first, I need a cup of coffee. Would you like one too?" They both nodded in agreement.

We arrived at the town center after 11 and found it swarming. The narrow streets were crowded with people and there was a sense of excitement in the air.

During the day, Mykonos seemed quite diverse, but at night, it seemed to have a predominantly gay crowd. "I'll never get a date tonight!" I said out loud. Roberto and Martino chuckled as we walked through the winding streets among the crowds. Eventually, we came across a bar/cafe where people had gathered to listen to live music. It was just a piano player, but the musician was rocking the place. As we approached the door, one of the female bartenders signaled to us. I turned around, thinking she was calling someone else, but then she motioned for us to follow her. The club was small, and every seat was occupied. I wondered where she could be leading us.

The piano was in the corner of an open floor set up like a stage. The waitress seated us right in front of the stage area, facing the piano player, who looked directly at us every time he looked up. At first, I felt uncomfortable as it seemed like we were under the spotlight. However, the attention soon shifted from the piano to a woman in her twenties with short blond hair and a round, friendly face, who walked out to the center of the "stage" with a microphone in hand. She welcomed everyone with a bow.

As she started to sing old hits by Carole King, James Taylor, and other vintage rockers, my mind wandered as I looked at the faces in the room. The light reflected off the floor, and everyone seemed enraptured in the music as they focused on the woman with the sweet voice.

I snapped back to reality as the singer paused, looked around the room, and began singing "Both Sides Now."

I had heard this Joni Mitchell song before but never experienced it like this. The words spoke of love, its illusions and about what I thought was real, but wasn't.

I couldn't help but wonder why it resonated with me so deeply. Somehow, her words cut through me and exposed my innermost thoughts and feelings. Memories of my past loves, romantic relationships, and aspirations for greatness all flooded back to me.

She continued relentlessly, as she sang of the dizzy feeling of falling in love, a sense of destiny in being with another, and then the disillusionment when it all falls apart. What I thought was love, she sang, was not.

As tears streamed down my face, Roberto leaned over and whispered, "Are you OK, Jovanny?" I nodded, but the truth was that I was not OK. The woman I had loved then left. The woman who loved me then left. Why? Because the magic was gone, the Ferris wheels stopped, the dancing froze, and June turned into October. Was my life magical or tragic? I couldn't help but think of all the people I had hurt by romancing them one minute, then sailing away the next, and how all of love's illusions had come crashing down.

As she continued, I could barely stand it.

She sang of life's illusions, of love, loss, certainty and doubt...I could relate to it all.

After she finished the song, I stood up, gave her a thumbs-up, blew her a kiss, and ran out onto the street.

When Roberto and Martino found me, I was sitting on the beach, gazing at the sea. By then, I had managed to calm myself down. They approached me and asked if everything was OK. I started sobbing when Martino put his arm around my shoulder and kissed my head. The strange thing is, I didn't know why. This sudden rush of emotions was a mystery to me. What did the words of that song pull from those depths of my being that made me so sad?

"Gio, we love you," Roberto said, trying to reassure me. But despite his efforts, his words only made me choke on my sobs. My two friends led me to a nearby tree trunk on the sand. They sat on either side of me, giving me time to work through my feelings. Through my tears, I caught a glimpse of the moon shimmering on the water, the silver waves gently patting the shore, and the night seagulls crying out to one another.

"I'm sorry," I said once I could speak. Both of my friends shook their heads, telling me not to worry. "I don't know why those words made me cry. I have no idea..." I trailed off, sobbing once again.

After a few minutes, my tears subsided, and Roberto whispered, "I think I understand why you're crying, my friend. It's because you feel the same pain that we all feel. You're hurting because you're not sure if your life has meaning. You want to be sure you're loved and capable of loving others. You want to know that your life has a purpose. You want to feel like you belong somewhere in someone's life. You want to know that the world is a better place because you're a part of it. Do you think I don't feel that way sometimes? But for me, it's easier because I have Martino. You have a life of adventures, but sometimes, maybe your heart yearns for a home."

Every damn word he said was true. Somehow, I was naked that evening on Mykonos; everyone could see what Jovanny was made of. I felt shame, like I needed to cover up my feelings and make light of them, but I couldn't. Not with these two. Not with my friends.

We spent a long time on the moonlit beach in the silence of each other's company. When the time came to leave, I was the first to stand up. "Thank you, my friends," I said with watery eyes. There was nothing more to say. Roberto and Martino hugged me, and we returned to our respective lodgings.

We spent a few more days on Mykonos together before we went our separate ways. However, that evening cemented our friendship in a way I cannot explain.

In the following weeks, months, and years, we sometimes kept in touch frequently, while at other times, we communicated less regularly, but we always picked up where we left off.

After meeting in Mykonos, Roberto and Martino invited me to visit them in Rome, which I did multiple times. They ran a bed and breakfast where I stayed, sometimes alone and sometimes with a girlfriend.

During one of my trips to Rome, Roberto and Martino recommended a gelato place they claimed was the best in the city. The only problem was that it was located on the other side of town, and I didn't have a car. Roberto and Martino had a Vespa, which could only carry two people. Nonetheless, they insisted that we go there because "only the best for our friends." Roberto made three trips to take us there: first, he took my then-girlfriend Silvia, then me, and finally Martino. The gelato place was a small, family-run business tucked away in an out-of-the-way location, and I would never have found it on my own. The gelato was good, but I wasn't sure if it was worth all the trouble. However, seeing Roberto and Martino's happy faces made it all worthwhile. "I'm so glad you're here, Gio," said Martino as he sat across from me, licking his cone.

Our lives have been running parallel for years after our time in Mykonos. Sometimes, they intersect, and other times, they move ahead, only to cross paths in the future and realize that our bonds are still strong.

When I'm sailing, I try to detach from the mainland, so I don't check my email or do any social media. Only Matteo has my emergency number. I like to find peace and focus on the adventure before me.

I had been sailing along the coast of Africa for a week when Matteo called me in the middle of the night. "My friend," he began, "Are you sitting down?" he asked. "Matteo, it's 2 in the morning; I am lying down. Is everything OK?" He assured me that he and his family were fine. "It's about your friends Roberto and Martino from Rome. Do you remember them?" I laughed. "Of course, Matteo. What happened?"

Matteo cleared his throat. "I don't know how to say this, Gio. Martino was killed in a motorcycle accident yesterday. I got a call this morning but wanted to confirm it before calling you." I don't know what I said after this; I remember trying to get off the phone. I was confused, incredulous, angry, and sad. What did I need to do, I wondered. As the minutes passed, I grew determined and focused; I got out of bed and turned my boat towards Italy.

By the time I got to Brindisi, packed my things, and got to Rome, the funeral had passed, and poor Martino had been buried. I was in shock, but I knew I had to focus on Roberto and offer him my support.

I found him working at his Airbnb, checking in guests, and performing his duties as usual. He seemed "normal," whatever that meant. He acted professionally, taking guests' documents, handing out keys, and sending them on their way.

When some guests lingered, he gestured for me to follow him into the kitchen, where I hugged him.

Roberto didn't show any emotion when I hugged him. After thanking me, we sat down and faced each other. I struggled to find the right words to say, "I'm so sorry." He responded, "Sorrow is not a big enough word for this." Roberto looked into my eyes before casting his gaze to the ground. We sat silently until he spoke again, "I'm just pretending to be alive. Inside, I'm dead. I'm only going through the motions of living because it seems like the right thing. Martino and I started this business, and I want to keep it going for him. But Gio, I don't know how I'll manage." At this point, he broke down, and I moved closer to him and put my arm around him as he wept, tears falling on the floor. This man, whom I had always admired for his strength and insight, was utterly broken. "I miss him so much," he sobbed. I replied, "I do, too," and added my tears to his. I missed Martino, but mostly, I missed seeing Roberto and Martino's smiling faces when they were together.

I had no words of consolation. I hoped that Martino could somehow see us now, could see how much he was still loved, and that his life was purposeful because he had discovered what mattered most.

When the weeping stopped, I looked at Roberto. His eyes were red, his mouth was drawn down, and his goatee dripped with tears. "My friend," I said, "come sailing with me, just you and me. I can't take away your sorrow, but I can offer you my friendship. Come sailing with me for a week, a month, a year. Please come sailing."

Roberto gazed at me for a while, trying to figure out what was behind my words. After a moment, he understood what I was trying to convey. "I won't say no; I can't tell you how many times Martino and I spoke about sailing with you..." He began to choke up again. "Then come," I said. "I will come, but not right now," he responded. "There are too many things to settle, and I don't want the business to fail."

Just at that moment, there was a knock at the door. It was a guest who was asking for restaurant advice. Roberto quickly snapped back to his old self and listed three or four restaurants within walking distance. As I watched him, I realized that, though wounded by grief, Roberto could pretend to be whole, at least for a while. I wondered if we all sometimes pretend to be whole when we are not.

After the guest left, Roberto asked me, "Gio, how long will you be in Rome? Can you stay through the weekend or even longer? I want us to have some time together." I replied, "As long as you need me, I am here."

"Please stay until mid-next week; after that, I have to settle Martino's affairs, promote the business, and take care of things I've been neglecting. Now, I have to clean the rooms and work on the accounts. Can we meet for dinner?"

I put my hand behind his neck, touched our foreheads, and left.

I eventually returned to my life in Brindisi and beyond. Roberto still hasn't taken me up on the sailing trip, but I know we will sail together when he is ready.

The mystery of Mykonos has continued. Roberto and I have a bond with one another that began with my tears and was sealed with his.

I often think of Roberto and Martino; I carry both in my heart.

# Chapter 10
# Risking Everything in Beirut

I must protect my friend's identity, so we will call him Charbel.

Friendship is how this story began.

Charbel was a software engineer in Beirut, but we met when he was on vacation in Tel Aviv. Those were my party days filled with clubbing, drinking, getting laid, and recovering at the beach. My friend Noam and I were familiar with all the popular hangouts, and we used to stay up all night and sleep during the day, almost like vampires.

We would often begin our evening at Rothschild Boulevard. One night, Noam and I met up with friends at one of the bars where we were regulars. "Another vodka, Cap?" the bartender asked me. I signaled with my thumb that I wanted another drink. About seven or eight of us were in a circle, sharing stories and having a good time, when I noticed a guy standing nearby. He was grinning and staring at our group, so I wondered if he was a nutcase.

Our eyes met briefly when I looked in his direction before he quickly looked away. I realized that he might feel left out or disconnected, so I decided to introduce myself. I left my group and walked over to him.

"Hello, I'm Jovanny," I said, extending my hand. And that's how we met. As we moved from one bar to another, Charbel joined our group. We laughed and had a great time until my stomach began to growl.

"I'm hungry," I announced. Noam chuckled and warned everyone, "Beware! When Jovanny is hungry, he gets annoyed with everything and everyone!" He knew me well.

While the others went to the next bar, Charbel joined me as I searched for a café. During my late meal of steak and eggs, Charbel talked about his life in Lebanon before the economic crash, his successful career, his close-knit family, and his friends. He seemed to be an optimistic and quality person. I also shared some details about my life up to that point; he was intrigued by the idea of living on a sailboat like many others. "It's not all fun and games," I recall saying. "It's a lot of hard work, and there's a lot of solitude at sea. It's not for everyone."

When I checked the time on my watch, I realized it was already past three, and I was starting to feel tired. So, I decided to head home instead of rejoining the others. "Are you free for a sail tomorrow?" I asked. Charbel's smile indicated a yes.

# Onward

Over the next few days, Charbel and I grew closer, and we have remained good friends for almost ten years. We have met up periodically, sometimes in Tel Aviv, other times in Cyprus, and once in Rhodes. Charbel is like family to me.

Fast forward to the last time we met.

After the big explosion in the port of Beirut in 2020, the country has been in total chaos. The blast brought to light corruption that people already knew about, but the world chose to ignore. Since then, there has been a surge in unemployment, hunger, protests, a drop in currency value, and governmental incompetence. The citizens are having a hard time finding food, shelter, and medical care in a crumbling healthcare system. The city of Beirut, once called the "Paris of the East," now looks like a city in decline.

Since we met in Tel Aviv, my friend has gotten married, settled in a nice area of Beirut, and had a son who is now four years old. He and his wife worked hard to save their money in dollars and deposited their savings into the largest Lebanese bank. They planned to use the funds to buy a house in Beirut's suburbs and create a wonderful life for themselves.

Unfortunately, three things happened that turned their lives upside down. Firstly, the economy collapsed, which caused Charbel to lose his job. Secondly, their son was diagnosed with cancer and needed expensive and prolonged treatments. Thirdly, the banks in Lebanon were in crisis.

When their son was diagnosed, the doctor said this particular form of cancer is treatable if caught in time, but Lebanon did not have the healthcare infrastructure. Through a series of contacts with the doctor's colleagues, the family decided to travel to Canada, where a medical center specializes in this form of childhood cancer. However, Charbel would need at least $150,000 to make this trip possible. Charbel was optimistic, knowing that they had already saved nearly $500,000.

Charbel called and told me part of the story that would unfold. "I was overjoyed when I learned that we had saved enough money for our son's treatment. I immediately went to the bank to withdraw the money, but to my shock, the bank manager claimed that they had no money. Confused, I asked again, but the manager repeated that they had no funds to let anyone withdraw and advised me to return the next week. I have been going there every day for two weeks, but the bank's response is always the same, and I cannot withdraw the money. My son's health is deteriorating, and we ran out of money for food. We have to rely on charity." At this point, Charbel began crying. When I asked how I could help, he said, "I will call you and let you know."

I wasn't aware of this situation in 2020. I had heard about the explosion but didn't keep up with the news. I also knew that Charbel's son had cancer and his family found a specialized hospital in Canada, but I didn't know that his assets were frozen.

# Onward

I was in Brindisi, taking a break from sailing, when Charbel called me again. His voice sounded worried, which was unusual for him. "Gio, my brother. I wouldn't ask you this if there was any other way, so please forgive me," he said. My heart started racing as I listened to him explain. "Do you trust me, Gio?" he asked. "With all my heart," I replied. "Can my wife and son stay with you in Brindisi until I arrive?" That was all he wanted? I was happy to help. "Of course," I replied. I could figure out how to house them. "Thank you, thank you, thank you, my friend," he said, his voice cracking. After a pause, he spoke again. "Gio, there's something else I need to ask you. Can you pick me up in Lebanon on your sailboat and bring me to Brindisi?" I didn't mind doing it, but I was curious. "Why don't you just fly?" I asked. "It's for my son's health," he said. "We need to get him treatment. Please trust me, my friend. I'll explain everything when we meet in person." I knew I had to help Charbel and his son. "Sure, just tell me what to do," I said. "I'll call you back in a few hours with more details," he said before hanging up.

Charbel called me only two hours later to inform me that his wife and son would arrive in Brindisi in four days. "Can you please set sail the same day they arrive, Jovanny?" I hadn't expected this to happen so soon, and I immediately made a list of things I needed to do to prepare the house and boat for my departure.

Fortunately, I had some local friends who were visiting their family in Egypt and offered their larger Brindisi home for me to use.

When I picked up Charbel's family at the airport, his wife seemed as clueless as I was. The only sure thing was that Charbel had informed her they would go to Canada for treatments within two weeks. He had a plan in mind that he was keeping from everyone.

After dropping them off at their lodging, I went to the marina to check on my boat. As I got onboard, Charbel called and revealed part of his plan.

He instructed me to leave the marina that evening and sail out to sea, following specific coordinates he gave me. Once I was there, he would rent a small boat from the marina and meet me at an agreed-upon rendezvous point out of sight of land. Once aboard my sailboat, we would sail to Brindisi, and from there, he would fly to Canada.

To my questions, "Why this? Why that?" he responded, "It is better that you not know, my friend. It is for your own good." This response was unusual for Charbel, who was typically laid back and open. Now, he appeared agitated, secretive, and desperate. "This is the only way to save my son, and I will not put you at risk. That is why I will not tell you the details. Just stay in the water at our rendezvous point until I get there. I might be late."

That was good enough for me.

# Onward

I decided to spend the rest of the afternoon preparing for the sail.

I departed from the marina at sundown and relied on the winds to reach my destination. Following Charbel's coordinates, I finally spotted the coast of Lebanon after spending days at sea. Following his instructions, I sent a one-letter message, a "C," to an unknown cell phone number to let him know I was in the area. I continued to our rendezvous point, located beyond the sight of land. Our agreement was that he would join me the next day.

After furling the sails, I tried to sleep but couldn't. I woke up the following day and waited, and waited, and waited. Then, I waited some more. Although I was tempted to call him, he had strictly instructed me not to contact him under any circumstances.

I kept looking towards the shore, hoping to see a sign of Charbel's arrival. Finally, in the late afternoon, I spotted a moving dot that gradually became a boat approaching. As it got closer, I could see Charbel waving at me. When his boat was about 50 feet away, I noticed a troubled expression on his face, which shocked me. "You made it!" I called out to him. "Thank you, Gio. But first, the bags. I will hand them to you," Charbel said, passing me four large, heavy canvas bags. I put the bags on the deck, and Charbel asked me to stow them below before he came up. I obliged.

When I returned to the deck and looked over, I saw Charbel using an ax to strike the bottom of the boat. "What the hell are you doing?" I asked. "I need to sink it," he replied. He made a hole so large that water began to rush in. Due to the engine's weight, the small boat started to tip. Charbel grabbed my ladder, climbed, and watched the motorboat sink completely. He continued climbing the ladder, jumped on board, hugged me, and started crying. "Thank you, my brother," he sobbed. "We have to leave for Brindisi now; I'll tell you the story when we're in Italian waters," he choked out.

As we sailed away from Lebanon, we said little to each other. Charbel sat on the deck, looking back. Was he bidding farewell to his land, or was he afraid of being followed?

While sailing past Greece, Charbel told me a story that made my hair stand on end.

"Do you have a gun, Gio?" he asked. I shook my head, and he continued, "I don't have one either. You know that I'm not a violent man. But I did something that you would never expect me to do." I gulped hard, waiting anxiously for him to continue.

"Gio, I love my wife and son and would do anything for them. You know this, right?" I nodded. "My son needs treatment to stop his cancer, and we have the money for his treatment, but the bank would not release my money. You know this also, right?" I nodded again. "Well, this is what happened, Gio. I came up with a plan I have not told anyone about, not even my wife. Do you want to hear about it?"

Uh, yeah.

"Through a friend of my uncle, I obtained a gun. Remember, Gio, that I don't even know how to shoot! I got this gun and six bullets; when the bank opened at ten o'clock, I entered and asked for the manager, who again refused to hand over my money. So I took out the gun, pointed it to his forehead, and shouted, 'This is a robbery! Everyone get down, or I will shoot him and you!' Yes, Gio, that is what I did," he said, looking at me as I shook my head incredulously.

"The manager stood there staring at me as if he didn't believe I would shoot; then I cocked the gun and pressed it hard against his temple. Fear crept across his face. I told him I needed all my money for my son's cancer and would kill him to save him. I think he believed me then. I told him that I would shoot him if the police arrived. So he nodded to his assistant, who got bags and started throwing dollars in. I told him I wanted everything; he said he could give me $120,000. I pressed the gun harder and told him yes, you have three minutes to put $120,000 in four bags without a transmitter or alarm. So that is what he did."

He paused in the middle of his story to sip water. I broke out into a cold sweat.

"I knew I had to leave the area before the police sealed it off; my description would be all over the media in a few minutes," Charbel explained. "So, I had arranged with a friend, who knew nothing of my plan, to leave the door unlocked to his shop but with the 'closed' sign in the window. The day before, I had gone to his shop and left a package for myself.

"Here's the funny part. I slipped into my friend's shop with four bags of money. First, I tied the bags with two ropes and dangled them from my neck so they were hanging in front of me. Then, I took a burka out of the box and put it on so you could only see my eyes. After that, I put on some women's sandals. Keep in mind that I did all this in two minutes or less. As I looked out the window, there was a lot of commotion outside. So, I just stepped out, bent over by the weight of the bags, and gradually strolled to the marina."

Charbel and I were both laughing at this point.

"I got into the boat, started the motor, and pulled out. Now, a person wearing a burka on a boat can draw attention. So this next part, Gio, promise me you won't laugh."

I couldn't promise.

"When I was away from the shore, I removed the burka and threw it into the water. I loosened the money bags and stowed them in the boat. Then I put on a woman's blouse that I had stashed on the boat and wore a big black wig with the hair dangling in front of my face."

At this point, I was crunched over and sank to the ground. The scene he described was too much for me.

"So there I was; imagine a beautiful black-haired woman steering her boat away from the shore. There were other boats around, but nobody paid any attention to me," he said.

"When I sighted your boat, I got rid of the wig and blouse; I didn't want to scare you off, Gio. And then, well, you know the rest."

After a simple dinner, we both went to bed exhausted from the stress and laughter.

I woke up in the middle of the night and started laughing again.

It wasn't until the next day that I realized the bravery of Charbel's actions and the risks he had taken.

Each friend, including me, played a part, but none was directly involved. If one part of the plan failed, Charbel would be in prison or worse, and his wife and son would be left with nothing in Brindisi.

My admiration for my friend grew that day.

When we arrived in Brindisi a few days later, Charbel's wife and son were waiting for us at the pier. Charbel hugged his wife and kids and cried while they tried to comfort him. His wife looked up at me, perplexed. Perhaps he would tell them someday.

"We fly tonight," he suddenly said, with wet eyes. "Tonight? But why?" his wife objected. "Please trust me," he responded. "I made our reservations from the boat," he said.

I said goodbye to them four hours later at the Brindisi airport. We agreed not to communicate until he reached Canada.

I found out afterward that Charbel had booked a series of flights through countries where tracking him would not be easy. The journey took over thirty hours, but I got a message five days later.

"Arrived. The cancer treatments begin the day after tomorrow. We are hopeful. I am so grateful. I am always your brother."

This time, I cried.

After four or five weeks, I heard from him again. "We have applied for asylum in Canada, and it looks like it will go through. We have a sponsor because of family here. The doctors are optimistic about the cancer going into remission. How can I thank you for helping my son?"

I don't know if I will see Charbel or his family again, but I do know that helping my friend rob a bank was one of the best things I've ever done.

# Chapter 11
# Tel Aviv and Jerusalem and Letting Go

I've been to Tel Aviv more times than I care to admit, drawn by its bars, clubs, beaches, and nightlife. A few bartenders knew me by name and would give me a free drink when I showed up again. Most of the time, I hung out with my friend Noam, who was a local. We had nicknames for each other: I was "Cap," short for captain, and he was "Pan," like Peter Pan, the boy who never wanted to grow up.

As I grew older, my interests changed, but Noam continued partying like he was in his twenties. Nonetheless, despite our differences, we remained close friends. However, I hadn't visited Tel Aviv in ages.

My journey back to Tel Aviv started in Crete. While sailing around Crete, I met Khalil and Yara at Voulisma Beach. "Do you live in Italy?" they asked me. "We've never been there, but maybe we'll visit you one day," Khalil said with a laugh. When I asked where they were from, they replied that they were from the Holy Land. Confused, I asked if they meant Israel. "We prefer 'Holy Land.' That way, we avoid politics," Yara said. We went to a cafe and spent the rest of the afternoon together.

"Have you been to the Holy Land?" Khalil asked. "Only Tel Aviv," I said. They looked shocked. "Then you have not seen our land at all," Khalil replied, shaking his head.

I turned to Yara and asked where she was from. "Bethlehem," they both said together.

I must have sounded silly because I asked, "THE Bethlehem? Christmas Bethlehem?" They both laughed. Yara explained that she grew up in Bethlehem but now lived near Khalil's family in Jerusalem. She worked in a tourist shop, and Khalil was an accountant.

We became good friends over the next few days, and I'm still grateful for our friendship.

The day before their flight home, Khalil said, "Gio, please visit us. I will show you Jerusalem, Bethlehem, and anywhere else you want to go. Please." I agreed after getting their promise that they would visit me in Brindisi.

This meeting happened four years ago, and now I'm preparing to return to Tel Aviv. I'll spend a few days with my friend Noam before traveling to Jerusalem to stay with Khalil and Yara.

Tel Aviv is a beautiful, modern, and sunny city with incredible beaches, lively bars, and visitors from all over the world.

# Onward

I asked Pan what he wanted to do this week after I got settled into his place. Noam, tall, slim, and a bit worn since we last saw each other, replied, "What we always do! Drink, party, and get laid," chuckling. My mind shifted to those years when Tel Aviv was my go-to place for all three. Pan and Cap, as the bartenders knew us, would often be out all night. But I cut back on my drinking when I turned thirty and strove to live a healthier lifestyle. "Gio!" Noam said to get my attention. "You with me here? You're daydreaming again!" I laughed. "Yes, my friend. I'll rest a bit. When do you want to head out?' When he said "midnight," I thought he was kidding. "I'm in bed by then!" I objected. "Not tonight, Gio. OK, let's head out at ten; does that work for you?" I agreed.

After a long nap and a quick dinner, we started at a rooftop bar near Rothschild's. Since it opened at 10:30, we were among the first customers. I could see that Noam was bored. "Do you want to go somewhere else and come back later?" I asked him. He gave me a thumbs-up, and we left.

We went to a fantastic place with outdoor tables surrounded by a vast garden. The place had a great vibe, with beer served in jars and a DJ playing excellent music. The indoor bar had two levels and was mostly filled with a young hipster crowd. As we sipped our beers and began to people-watch, I remarked, "It's a young crowd, but I like the atmosphere." Noam clinked my glass and replied, "Too young for you, but not for me. Do you remember Charbel? He used to be a magnet with the ladies. Why did he have to go off and get married?" Noam sighed.

We watched but didn't flirt, content to be with each other and observe the world around us. Noam pointed towards a beautiful but very young woman standing by the bar and asked, "What do you think of her?" I replied, "Too young." A few minutes later, he nodded towards another woman. "Young," I said. When an American-looking woman walked by, Noam winked at her. She smiled and kept walking. He looked at me inquisitively. "Young," I replied. He laughed and said, "Come on, my friend, let's find some grandmas for you."

It was like sardines when we returned to the rooftop bar around 1 am. I had already consumed three drinks and had switched to water as I had reached my limit. "Come on, Cap! Have one more drink! Don't become the old man on my watch!" he scolded, but I remained firm. We found a spot where we could see the entire room. When I leaned against the wall and yawned, Noam exclaimed, "Don't you dare!" I shrugged.

By 2 a.m., I was ready to leave, but Noam was starting to work the room. "Noam, I'm heading home; I can't keep my eyes open. You stay and have fun," I said, yawning again. My friend looked crestfallen and tried to convince me to stay. "I see five or six girls just your type, Gio! You're going to miss out!" he complained. I stretched out my hand for the keys, hugged Noam, and left.

Onward

I decided to walk home since he didn't live far and I wanted to clear my head.

What had changed for me? Was I getting old?

There was a time when I would long to return to Tel Aviv for the three reasons that Noam stated: drinking, partying, and getting laid. But even sex had become more complicated since my love affair in Dubrovnik. Somehow, "getting laid" wasn't enough since sex had more meaning now. Was that a sign of getting old? I was too tired to figure it out.

I crashed in his guest room and slept about four or five hours until the sun came up. Since sailing regulates my life, I am used to waking up early, typically at dawn, and going to bed by ten. I got up and looked for the coffee pot in the kitchen. Noam's door was wide open, so I took a peek inside to see if he wanted some coffee, but his bed hadn't been slept in.

I brewed some coffee, grabbed my cup, and crawled back into bed to start my day nice and easy. Then, all of a sudden, I heard the front door open and figured Noam had come back. Not sure if he was alone, I decided to stay in my room while he went into his room and shut the door.

After taking a shower, I headed to Gordon Beach, where I planned to spend most of the day. I left Noam a note to meet me there later.

Gordon Beach is probably the busiest beach in Tel Aviv, and even though it was only 11 a.m., it was already buzzing. I walked across the sand and had to dodge bikes, a cafe on the sand, and twenty-something-year-olds partying in groups. The water was my goal, and I kept my gaze on the beautiful turquoise waves ahead of me.

I found a locker to secure my wallet, ran to the water, and dived in. The feeling was amazing; a warm caress surrounded me, and I felt secure and wanted for nothing. I swam away from the crowds into the blueness, feeling like I was between the waters and the sky, belonging to both and neither. Here, I found "my" Tel Aviv.

After three or four hours, I headed to the locker to get my phone and wallet before walking to the volleyball courts further down the beach. Noam had not messaged me, so I decided to eat.

I was starving and found a beach cafe where I ordered a falafel plate, which included spicy fried falafel balls, salad, pickles, tahini, and pita bread. After finishing my meal with a glass of sparkling water, I ordered the shakshuka - poached eggs nestled in a spiced tomato stew. I don't know how many pitas I ate, but I wanted to soak every drop of the sweet, slightly spicy tomato sauce.

Not feeling ready to lie on the beach, I watched some volleyball games after paying my bill. Some tournament was going on between I don't know who and I don't know what. All the players seemed twenty-some years old and took the sport very seriously.

Suddenly, a blonde woman approached me and asked, "Excuse me, would you like to play? We need another player." She looked stunning in her bikini with her long blonde hair and green eyes. I must have looked like a fool as I stared at her and nodded in agreement.

She led me to another group of people playing volleyball for fun rather than sport. "What's your name?" she asked as we walked. "Jovanny. My name is Jovanny," I stuttered. She giggled as if she understood why I was stumbling. After an awkward silence, I asked for her name. I expected her response to be "Perfecta. My name is Perfecta, but my friends call me Perfect." Instead, she said, "Sofia." When I asked her where she was from, she said, "Estonia." "We are from all over the world here," she continued as we met the other teammates. "This is Jovanny, from?" she asked. "California and Brindisi," I said. We got down to business after shaking a few hands and exchanging names.

Soon, my competitive side emerged as I dove, spiked, and slammed the ball. "Jovanny!" Neil, my teammate from New Zealand, called out as I hit the ball towards him, and he pushed it over the net. We now had our strategy; I hovered towards the back to cover my teammates. "Jovanny!" Sofia called as I passed her the ball. Perfecta made a perfect slam, and we were soon killing our opponents. "Losers buy the beer," someone called out. That was a great idea, as I dove into the sand and saved the ball. Another teammate put it over the net.

Our victory was so swift that we decided to go for two out of three, but we defeated our opponents a second time, so a third game wasn't necessary. "Three out of five, come on!" Neil shouted out. Everyone agreed.

We huddled up to discuss strategy. "Why don't we let their team win one," Jude from Nigeria suggested. It seemed ridiculous; I didn't know how to lose on purpose. But I kept my mouth shut and played.

"Hey, don't be like that!" someone from the opposing team called out when they realized we were intentionally losing. Before this match, we hadn't missed any shots; however, now my team was either hitting the ball out of bounds or missing it entirely. "Come on, guys, let's play!" I urged my team. We refocused our efforts, employed our strategy, and ultimately won the game.

Beer time!" Neal exclaimed. "Thanks, Jovanny! You're coming, right?" Jude asked. "Sure, I just need to check my messages," I replied.

Meanwhile, the others had already started walking towards a nearby beach bar. When I looked up from my phone, I realized my team had left. I read a text from Noam, "I'm on my way to the beach; let's meet in front of the Sheraton."

When I reached Noam, he looked terrible - pale, mouth agape, and exhausted. "Don't say it," he said. "I know I look like shit. I have a terrible hangover, and I feel as bad as I look," he added. I patted him on the back and took him to a café where we could grab something. However, I frowned when he ordered a bloody Mary. "It's the only thing that will make my splitting headache disappear," he explained, reading my expression. "But it'll only push it until tomorrow," I replied. "But I'm not your mother," I added. "Yes, I know. If you were my mother, you'd repeat the same thing again and again. Thank you for not being my mother," he joked. I ordered a Gazoz, a fruity lemonade, and a plate of hummus and pita. "Come on, eat!" I said, pushing the plate towards Noam. "I can't," he replied, sipping on his drink. "At least have some fruit?" I suggested. He nodded and ordered a fresh fruit plate.

As my friend started to look human again, I asked him what he wanted to do. It was already four o'clock. "Nothing," he replied. "What does 'nothing' mean?" I asked. "Lay on the beach, soak up the sun, relax. Then we can hit the clubs later on." I laughed, as we were obviously on entirely different pages. "I'll relax with you on the beach, but no clubs for me tonight. I'm going to hang out here," I said. I had found my Tel Aviv, and standing around a bar trying to hook up or watching my friend try didn't sound like a good time. Noam raised his glass in agreement, and we both turned to gaze at the water.

Suddenly, a woman's voice interrupted us from behind. "Jovanny! What happened to you?" I turned and saw Sofia walking towards us, wearing a sheer shirt over her bathing suit. I stood up and introduced her to Noam, who just sat there and stared. "I came here to visit my friend, who rose from the dead this afternoon," I replied, laughing. Sofia disappeared into the crowd, promising to be back soon. "Gio! What have I just seen?" Noam babbled. When I explained that I had played volleyball with her and her friends, he continued, "You gotta go for it, Gio! I mean, she likes you! Don't let that one slip through your fingers! She wants you! You're a fool to let that one go!" He stopped talking when Sofia returned. "This is Sebastian, my fiancé," she said, introducing her companion. He was at the same level: chiseled face, muscled body, blond hair, big hands as he reached out to shake ours. "Please," I said, inviting them to sit with us.

As Noam remained silent and continued staring, I said, "Don't mind him. He's hungover and can't deal with reality yet." Everyone chuckled except Noam. "I'm glad you're here. But where are the others?" I asked. Sofia smiled and replied, "I enjoy playing volleyball, but everyone on the team is much younger. They're excited because they're having their first beers, dates, or whatever. I'm over that, so I called Sebastian, and here we are!" I glanced over at my friend. "Noam, say something!" I urged. He blinked and responded robotically, "It's so nice to meet both of you."

Sofia took the lead and asked about our lives and where we were from. Noam was pretty useless, in a daze as he ordered another bloody Mary. "I live in Brindisi like I told everyone at the game, but my real home is my sailboat," I said. Sofia's eyes grew wide, and Sebastian was suddenly engaged. "How are you able to do that?" he asked. I didn't know how to respond; after a minute, I said, "I just decided that's how I wanted to live my life. I got a boat and have been figuring it out ever since. Have you sailed?" I asked him. "Just a few times, but Sofia and I have been talking about going on a sailing adventure, and here you are, living an adventure all the time!" he exclaimed. Sofia glanced at him and smiled. "Do you want to come out with me on the boat?" I asked. Noam groaned; perhaps it was the thought of seasickness. "Is tomorrow morning too soon?" Sofia asked. I laughed. "Not at all. Tomorrow morning, 9 o'clock at the pier," I replied.

Sebastian turned to Noam. "Can your friend come too?" he kindly asked. I answered for him: "No fucking way."

We said our goodbyes until the next day, and Noam soon finished his drink. "Let's hang out for a while," he said.

Noam rented a beach lounge while I dove into the water and swam beyond the crowds again. Hours passed, and the cafes began turning on their lights as the sun was setting. The water took on a pink hue, reflecting the clouds. I floated there, admiring the beautiful seafront and grateful for my time in Tel Aviv.

When I returned, Noam was still asleep in his lounge chair, so instead of disturbing him, I sent him a message and went to his apartment to shower and rest.

Matteo called me while I was at the apartment and asked, "How is Tel Aviv treating you, my friend?" I chuckled and replied, "I think I'm turning into an old man! There are so many clubs here that I've lost count of them; the nightlife never ends, and there are girls everywhere! But I only want to hang out at the beach and go to bed early." There was a brief pause before Matteo responded.

"I have a mask that looks exactly like me, Gio. My wife will never suspect a thing. Let's switch places. There's a flight leaving at midnight. Then you can have all your home life, and I can party." He said all this with his deadpan voice, so I took up the thought. "Ryanair arrives at 6 a.m. in Brindisi; pick me up, put the mask on me, and then you take the next flight for Tel Aviv. Oh, and tell your wife you won't have sex with her for a while because you have a rash." Matteo laughed. "No worries, Gio. She has a rash, too, so that is no problem."

With that, we said goodbye and hung up.

By 9 p.m., I was getting restless at the apartment, so I sent Noam a message, put on my bathing suit under my shorts, and headed out.

I noticed some surfers at Hilton Beach, so I inquired if I could rent a surfboard at night. The area was bustling with swimmers, party-goers, and tourists. After waiting in line for five minutes, I met a group of guys who were also night surfers. After securing my phone, I got my board and joined them in the water.

"Hey guys, this is Jovanny!" one shouted. "Hey Jovanny, I'm Gil!" said another, and the rest of the group introduced themselves. Surfing at night is risky, so we agreed to keep an eye on each other. Each of us partnered up with someone and watched them ride their wave before taking our turn.

Although the swells were small, they were enough to catch a few runs. However, what made the experience memorable was not our surfing skills but the breathtaking scenery that surrounded us. The lights from the nearby cafes reflected on the water, the sky glittered with millions of stars, and the full moon created an eerie glow on my board.

As we surfed in the warm waters of Tel Aviv, some of the guys let out yelps of excitement when they caught a wave or even when they wiped out. I tried my best not to yelp, but a cry or two did escape. "Good job, Jovanny!" one of my companions shouted as I caught a wave that brought me almost to the shore. "Way to go, Les!" another called out to a friend.

Though we had spoken little, our camaraderie was strong when we all headed to shore after midnight. As we stood in a circle on the beach, none of us wanted to leave. "You guys want to grab a beer?" one asked. When everyone agreed except me, I had the whole group on my back. "Come on, Jovanny! ONE beer! You can't go home yet! Just ONE!" They wore me down. "OK, just one. Well, maybe two!" They all clapped.

Tel Aviv was a youthful city, so it was no surprise that everyone in the group was in their twenties except for me. I saw my younger self in their faces, eagerly exploring Tel Aviv for adventure.

We ended up in a noisy bar and shared exaggerated surfing stories from the evening, multiplying the tiny wave we had surfed into a twenty-footer we dreamed about. When someone asked about my background, I told them about my sailboat life, and suddenly all eyes were on me. Interestingly, people from all backgrounds find my nomadic life appealing. "Jovanny, what's the best place you've surfed?" I laughed as my mind went back and forth. "Senegal was amazing, but the surfing in Morocco was unforgettable. I swear, Morocco is a surfer's paradise."

Prodded for more details, I shared my experience. "Taghazout is among the top surfing destinations in the world. It has a cool hippie atmosphere and isn't expensive at all. It has areas for all levels of surfers. My favorite is Anchor Point, discovered by Australians in the 60s. The point is a thumb of rock that juts out, where the take-off is tight because it draws a huge number of surfers who compete for space. So you are suddenly taken by a fast and challenging peak that plunges you into a steep section where you have to nail the turn just in time. After that, you're in an area called the roller coaster, which draws on every ounce of your skill and stamina. It can be a scary but incredible ride," I concluded. There was a brief pause before Les, a capable surfer, proposed, "Hell, why don't we go? Let's make it happen!" Others chimed in and agreed.

After we raised our glasses and cheered for the possibility, one of the guys asked, "Jovanny, do you think we could handle Anchor Point?" I nodded. "I have a friend who runs a fantastic hostel there. He is well-connected in the surfing community. If you guys are serious, I can contact him at some point. Yes, we can do it. I can easily arrange it. But what about you guys, with work, girlfriends, and car payments?" They laughed.

I grew tired and sleepy, but before I left, we exchanged contact numbers and agreed to meet again at Anchor Point the following year, no matter what.

After rinsing off at the beach, I walked to Noam's place, climbed the stairs, entered my room, and crashed on the bed until morning.

When I woke up, my muscles were sore, but I was always up for a good sail. I drank my coffee, took a shower, grabbed some food, and left the apartment without checking on Noam. He was probably asleep in his bed or someone else's.

I arrived to find Sofia jumping up and down while Sebastian sat relaxed. "Is anyone excited about sailing?" I asked. After kissing me on the cheek, Sofia replied, "Beyond words." Sebastian added, "Believe it or not, I'm excited, but my caffeine hasn't kicked in yet." "No worries," I said. "I have a coffee maker on board, so we can continue waking up there. Are you ready to head over to the pier? Did you bring some food?" They nodded. "I have some supplies on board, but I'm going to grab some sandwiches near the dock," I added.

After prepping the boat, we set sail from Tel Aviv. Sebastian sipped his coffee and relaxed while Sofia was energetic and excited. She couldn't get enough of the views or the sensation of being on the water. "I wish I could harness her energy into the wind," I joked, as the breeze was gentle and we moved slowly. Sofia turned and squinted at us. "Ha ha," she said sarcastically. Suddenly, a sharp wind caught the sail and jerked the boat. Sofia almost toppled over as we lunged forward. She braced herself and exclaimed, "This is sooooooo cool."

The day's sail should be easy as we headed north towards Haifa while hugging the coast. Our journey started by passing Herzliya, a wealthy community on a serene beach. A few people were relaxing on the sand, but nobody responded when Sofia waved. "Stuck-up rich people," she muttered. Sebastian teased her by saying, "Someone is jealous." Sofia quickly denied it by saying, "No way! I would never want to be like them! I would only want to own a house there but not talk to them!"

As we approached Caesarea, we all got excited, even Sebastian. I brought the boat as close to the shore as possible, and we floated by the excavated ruins of the ancient harbor of King Herod, the Roman amphitheater, a castle, and the remains of a Crusader church. "The city was built by King Herod over 2,000 years ago!" Sebastian exclaimed. "You mean King Herod, who had all the babies slaughtered when he thought that a king was born who would take his place?" Sofia asked. "The same," Sebastian replied. "Such beauty and horror in the same place," Sofia said. We watched tourists wandering among the ruins and up the theater's stairs. Sebastian revealed himself to be a history buff as he continued. "An inscription bearing the name of Pontius Pilate was found here, which indicates that he ruled from this area. It is named Caesarea to honor Caesar Augustus, but that name came from King Herod, who was trying to play both fields: a Jewish leader with Roman power. But, in the end, he is remembered as the guy who murdered babies because he didn't want to lose his throne."

After a pause, I added, "There is an incredible underwater museum here where you can go down and explore the submerged ancient city. You can rent the gear in the city, which I've always wanted to do. Maybe we can plan for it on our next visit," I said after a brief pause. Sofia seemed interested and asked, "Where is it? Are we above it now?" I replied, "No, it's further out from here."

As we sailed, we approached some of the country's most beautiful beaches. A Roman aqueduct that extended to the water caught our attention, and we saw only a few people in the water. Sofia asked, "Where is everyone?" I shook my head, reminding her, "It isn't Tel Aviv."

We sailed until noon as the sun rose higher in the sky. Feeling hungry, I suggested that we take a break and have some snacks. Sebastian and Sofia immediately jumped up, and within five minutes, they laid out a delicious spread of chilled wine, cheese, hummus, fruits, and sliced meats. I was surprised at how quickly they had put it all together. "Where did all that come from?" I asked, laughing. Sebastian nodded towards Sofia as she filled three glasses with a superb sparkling wine. We raised our glasses and toasted to our adventure.

"Jovanny, how long will you stay in Tel Aviv?" asked Sofia. "Tomorrow, I'm heading to Jerusalem," Without skipping a beat, she asked, "Why?" "I want to see the city and visit my friends there." She responded, "I would never want to be part of that world." Now it was my turn; "Why?" The conversation caught the attention of Sebastian, who leaned in to listen. "Because it is so...religious. Depressing. So serious. So ridiculous." I didn't mean to challenge her, but I wondered where she gathered these impressions. "So you have been there?" I asked. Sofia was silent, and Sebastian didn't say anything. "I've just heard about it," Sofia finally replied. "This will be my first time," I continued. "I want to experience the history, culture, and people. Tel Aviv has been great, but I want to see more. Plus, my friend Khalil and his wife Yara live there." "That makes sense," Sofia responded.

# Onward

We eventually had to turn the boat around because the winds could be unpredictable, and I wanted to arrive in Tel Aviv before evening.

The three of us were quiet during the first part of our return trip. It was as if the topic of Jerusalem introduced a dose of reality into the dream-like experience we had been having. Suddenly, Sebastian asked, "Do you like Tel Aviv?" I replied, "That's a great question, Sebastian. I've been visiting Tel Aviv for a decade and have always enjoyed it. The bars and party scenes are amazing. Strangely enough, they are still amazing, but I enjoyed them less this time. I guess Tel Aviv hasn't changed, but maybe I have."

"It's a young city," Sofia said. "It's great for someone fresh out of college, but the city itself never seems to mature, don't you think?" She sat down beside Sebastian, who wrapped his arm around her. "But we do grow up, don't we?" she said, lost in thought.    After we finally parked the boat at the marina, we were too wiped out from being roasted by the sun to make any plans to meet up later. So, we shared our contact info, hugged each other, and said our goodbyes before heading our separate ways.

When I arrived home, I didn't bother checking if Noam was in his room. I went straight to my bed and crashed. When I awoke at around 9 pm, he still wasn't around, so I sent him a message, grabbed my things, and went down to the beach for food and a night swim. A few hours later, I received a message from Noam inviting me to meet him at a bar around midnight.

"I'm wiped from my sail today; heading to bed. See you in the morning before I leave," was my reply.

A sense of sadness washed over me when I woke up the next day. While making coffee and waiting for Noam to wake up, I realized that leaving Tel Aviv meant leaving a part of myself behind. The train to Jerusalem was scheduled for noon, but I dreaded it. I wasn't just leaving my friend Noam; I was leaving a part of myself. The carefree, live-for-the-moment vibe of Tel Aviv had suited me for years, but now I found myself questioning everything. Why didn't I feel the same way as Noam?

Sitting on the balcony, sipping my coffee under the morning sun, I had more questions than answers.

When Noam finally got up and slumped into a chair on the balcony, coffee in hand, he asked me if I had enjoyed myself the past few days. "It was great, my friend," I replied. I almost added, "But I wish we had spent more time together," but I stopped myself, not wanting to feel obligated to go out bar hopping all night the next time I visited. "I love the water here, and I could spend all day at the beaches," I continued. "Besides, Noam, your friendship means a lot to me," I added.

Noam appeared tired and drained as he gazed out at the water. "Do you think you will make it through Jerusalem?" he inquired, to which I chuckled and responded, "There's always a first time for everything!" Noam, my loyal friend who always supported me, suggested, "If you find it too difficult, you can always return here. The guest room is yours, and I love having you here."

My taxi was honking downstairs, so I grabbed my bag and hugged Noam. He saw that I was teary-eyed. "Awww, Gio, always the sentimental one! That's why I love you!" he said as he kissed my cheek.

Walking downstairs and climbing into the taxi, I said goodbye to something I could not yet define.

I got on the train and found myself in another world in about thirty minutes: Jerusalem.

When I got to the Jerusalem station, it was like I landed in the future instead of an ancient city. The station was sleek, modern, and polished, with tranquil piano music in the background. It's a remarkable engineering feat because the train runs eighty meters underground, which makes it one of the deepest train lines in the world.

Since I traveled light, I was able to quickly navigate the dozen or so escalators that took me to the top. The station was buzzing with people, including backpackers, kids chatting away, tourists, and locals. I hoped I blended in with my baseball hat, jeans, and T-shirt.

When I stepped into the fresh air, Khalil and Yara were already waiting for me at the top of the last escalator. Both of them were wearing shorts and tank tops. Yara, who used to be a brunette, now had contrasting blonde hair and dark eyes. She handed me a sunflower and shouted, "Gio! Welcome to Jerusalem!"

We hugged each other with huge smiles, so much so that I thought my face might crack. Khalil exclaimed, "We are so glad you are here, my friend!" Yara added, "It's all he's been talking about for months. 'Gio is coming in a few months,' or 'Do you think Gio will like this?' He's been driving me crazy! But I'm happy you're here too!" she said, laughing.

"Where's Jerusalem?" I asked, looking around. Everything around us was new. "That's what's so great about our city," Khalil said. "The new and old are mixed together, shaken up, and form a wonderful whole!" Yara added, "But don't worry, wait until you get to our house if you want to see old!"

When our tram arrived, we hopped on and journeyed back thousands of years into East Jerusalem, where Khalil's family has owned a large stone home for generations.

It was a strange experience traveling from the mainly Jewish part of the city, with its smooth and well-kept roads and tidy buildings, to the eastern, more Arab part, where the infrastructure seemed neglected and shabby. Yara sensed my thoughts and said, "Now you will experience life in two worlds." I asked, "Do you mean Tel Aviv and here?" She shook her head and replied, "No, I mean two worlds in one city. You will see."

We got off the tram and hiked down a few winding streets until we arrived in front of a large gray stone building. Although the building looked like it needed some repairs, it was magnificent. "This is my family's home, where we will be staying," Khalil said.

Khalil stepped forward, opened the grand front door, and gestured for me to step in. As soon as I entered, I was greeted by around twenty family members and friends who welcomed me with loud cheers of "Welcome, Gio!" I was so surprised that I couldn't say anything, so I stood there feeling awkward. Khalil then put his arm around my shoulder and said, "Gio, you are now a part of our world, home, and lives. Welcome to our family."

Once inside, everyone formed a circle around us, and as I thanked them, my voice faltered.

Khalil and Yara then hugged me and led me to the dining room, where the family had arranged a table full of delicious food. Looking around, I could feel the warmth and love in the room. "I wish I had come earlier," I said, my voice choking with emotion. "You were always welcome here," Yara replied, kissing me on the cheek.

"Hey Mama!" Khalil called out as a middle-aged woman with black hair and dark eyes, wearing a silver cross around her neck, approached me. "This is Gio. Gio, this is my mother, Mariana!" Mariana smiled and took my hands, saying, "We are so happy you have come, Gio," while looking into my eyes. Khalil then suggested I relax for a minute or wash up before eating. "Let me show you to your room," he said, leading me upstairs to a large room with wooden floors, white plaster walls, and a window with a great view of the city. "This is your room, my friend," he said, showing me the bathroom with everything I needed.

"Gio, about the bathroom. We have had plumbing problems for years, but the government will not permit us to do the repairs. So the water pressure is very low. You can take a shower downstairs, where there is more pressure. For a bath, we have a system to carry up the water. Whatever you prefer," he said.

"What do you mean you can't get a repair permit?" I asked. He gestured for me to take a seat while he settled in the other chair.

"Doing any work on older buildings requires a permit. However, if you're an Arab family living in East Jerusalem, getting a permit is really tough. If you do the repairs anyway, you'll get a building violation notice from the government. And if you're Palestinian, they might even demolish your home. These rules, and a lot of other things, create a lot of pressure on Palestinian families, pushing them to sell their homes and leave. It seems like the government wants to make life as hard as possible for us, hoping we'll eventually give up and move. But let's not dwell on this! I want you to enjoy your time here. For the rest, well, you'll draw your own conclusions."

Khalil got up and asked, "I will see you in about half an hour?" I gave him a thumbs-up.

I lay down for a while, but the smell of roasting meat wafting through my room soon told me it was time to go downstairs. Yara called out my name and said, "I hope you are hungry!" She whispered, "If you are not, just pretend because Khalil's mom will watch you eat!" and laughed. She led me to the dining area where everyone had gathered. The table was big enough to seat about twenty-five people. Khalil introduced me to his father, Michel, a strong-looking, stout man with short-cropped, graying hair and a small goatee. He took my hand, pulled me towards him, and gave me two solid kisses on each cheek. "Thank you for coming, Gio," he repeated.

I felt like an imposter. Maybe they mistook me for someone else? Did they assume that I was some celebrity in disguise? I was pleased to meet them, but they seemed overjoyed to meet me.

After a while, everyone held hands, and the father of the family led the group in a prayer of blessing. I looked across the room at a picture of the Madonna and child on one wall and the Pope on another. "Amen!" everyone said together.

I knew my friends were Palestinian Christians, but I didn't know what that meant to them. But I was OK with it all.

One plate after another started to arrive from the kitchen: hummus and Baba Ghanoush served with flatbread, giant bowls of salads of tomato, cucumber, onion, bell peppers, lemon juice, and tahini. A few minutes later, Khalil's father, Michel, came in carrying giant skewers of kabobs. "Chicken, beef, or lamb, or all three!" he said with a smile. Then came the falafel, followed by red peppers stuffed with tomatoes, olives, feta, rice, and other dishes I couldn't even count. I hadn't eaten much that day, so I had no problem with anything they put in front of me.

"Gio, you must come again and often!" Michel said as he lifted his wine for a toast. Glasses clinked as one after another said, "To Gio!" I again wondered what they saw in me. I raised my glass and said, "Thank you for your wonderful hospitality, all of you, and to Khalil and Yara, my dear friends." Glasses clinked again. Michel stood up; he looked at me and then at his wife. "You are like another son, yes Maria?" he said as Maria nodded. "Whenever you come, you have your room here and your family."

Looking around the table at the smiling and chatty faces, I felt grateful to be there. It was then that I realized Khalil must have informed his parents about the death of mine, and their warm welcome now made sense. Khalil patted me on the back and winked as if sensing my thoughts.

"Gio, how are you?" Yara asked, leaning over. I smiled and responded with a question. "Yara, where is your family?" She whispered her response, "My family lives in Bethlehem, and it's not easy for them to come to Jerusalem. But we're going there tomorrow, and they insisted on making lunch for you. But don't worry, Gio, that will be the last family event we'll force you into!" I thanked her and said I was looking forward to it.

Three or four conversations were happening simultaneously at the table. Michel signaled with his finger on his lips when Youseff, Khalil's older brother, brought up Israeli politics. "No politics allowed at the table is my father's rule," Khalil whispered.

"Gio! Please tell us about your adventures," Khalil's cousin Amira asked. I chuckled. "Which one?" I replied. Suddenly, everyone's attention was on me. "Alright, do you want to hear about my boat almost sinking, when I almost got arrested in Algeria, or when I sailed down the Nile with my friend?" Algeria was the winner, so I did my best to retell how tiny I felt in the universe there, leaving the "almost arrested" part for the end.

Khalil shook his finger when Youseff asked if I would take him as my first mate. "I will always be the first mate," he said. "You both did pretty well when we sailed from Brindisi up the coast," I said. The year after we met, Khalil and Yara had visited me and sailed along the Italian coast from Brindisi. It seems like last week. "All of you are welcome on my boat," I told the group. "But not all at the same time; it's small, but it's waiting for us in Tel Aviv."

Immediately, Khalil's siblings and cousins pleaded to accompany me to Tel Aviv. I laughed and said, "Yes, come all. But I will let Khalil organize it." He laughed and responded, "That is the most difficult job, Gio, and I will make many enemies here."

Youseff asked, "Do you take bribes, brother?" Khalil responded, "Yes."

Toward the end of the meal, Yara suggested that we explore the old city before it got too late. We thanked everyone for the beautiful food and companionship before leaving.

"You will see sorrowful and happy places," Khalil said as we headed towards the Church of the Holy Sepulchre. We passed by the Pools of Bethesda and crossed over the Via Dolorosa. A religious service was going on outside, led by a Franciscan, and it might have been the stations of the cross. We paused to listen briefly as the priest said, "Simon steps out of history and helps Jesus carry the cross. He disappears after playing his part, but his choices that day ripple down to us. He helped Christ, and for that, we remember him. We, too, have a role to play. But what will our role be, and how will our choices ripple through others' lives…"

Yara nudged Khalil, who then caught my attention, and we slipped out of the small crowd and down a side street.

Upon arriving at the Church of the Holy Sepulchre, I felt transported back in time. The building's old, weathered stone exterior cannot conceal its grandeur, a mixture of a fortified church and a castle from the time of the Crusades. The doors were wide open, as if to welcome everyone.

The church's interior is more like a labyrinth than a traditional place of worship, with hidden passageways, small chapels, and stairs leading in all directions. Many people were taking photographs, while others were exploring the church. However, we had a specific purpose. Khalil motioned for us to follow him up the stairs. "We will begin with sorrow," he said as he led us into a chapel with a large painting of the crucifixion. "This is Golgotha, where Jesus was crucified," Yara whispered.

Although some visitors seemed more interested in taking selfies than in prayer, I did my best to ignore them and cherish the moment.

Yara was the first to kneel, but Khalil and I joined her. Although I lost the habit of praying years ago, I found myself thanking God for my life and asking for help for Yara and Khalil and their families.

Our moment of peace was interrupted by a large tour group entering the area, so we got up and headed downstairs. Khalil then remarked, "Now for joy," and we walked to the center of the church, under the dome, where we found a big stone rectangular box. "That is the tomb where Jesus rose from the dead," Yara said. "It doesn't look like a tomb," I blurted out. "Just the slab is original," Khalil answered. "The rest was added in the 19th century to mimic a tomb's form. The area had been leveled out by removing tons of earth and rock, and a church had been built to incorporate both the events of the crucifixion and resurrection. "To contain both the sorrow and the joy," I added, and Khalil nodded in agreement.

As the line to the tomb was too long, we decided to move on.

We left through a side door and walked towards the Temple's western wall.

As we approached the Temple, Khalil noticed that Yara was wearing shorts, which meant she couldn't enter the area. "I will stay here with her; you go ahead. Take your time; we will sit over there and people-watch." I started to say, "But...", then Yara responded, "It's fine, Gio. We have seen it many times. You go and experience its history; see if the wall speaks to you." I nodded and then, reluctantly, left them to enter the Temple area.

I put on my paper yarmulke and approached the Western Wall. As I looked around, I saw people of all types: some were praying, others seemed to be reflecting, and some were tourists like me, exploring and looking around. As I walked up to the wall, I touched the stones. Notes and papers were stuffed between the rocks, filled with prayers and petitions from those who hoped to be heard by the divinity. I didn't pray because the wall didn't speak to me that way, but I could feel its history. The Temple was built by King Herod and destroyed by the Romans during a time when the local Jewish population was oppressed and dispersed throughout the world. Today, the ruined Temple is a sorrowful symbol of past conflict and oppression.

I began to wonder what the visitors were praying for. Were they praying for peace and happiness, a united Israel and Palestine, or neither? Were they sick and hoping for a cure? Did they have a child that needed help?

# Onward

As I left the area, I felt sad. It was as if the broken temple signaled a broken humanity.

My friends and I locked arms and headed towards the Mount of Olives lookout.

The sun was setting, so Khalil urged us to hurry before dark. We wanted to avoid the tour groups and find a more secluded spot to gaze upon the City of Peace. Luckily, Yara found a perfect place for us. The dimming light reflected off the Dome of the Rock, and the city below seemed to glow. Excitedly, Khalil pointed to a jumble of buildings and asked if I could see his home. I fibbed and said yes.

"In one view, you see Jerusalem's wonder and problems," he continued. "The Dome of the Rock in the middle of the remains of the Jewish Temple, both forever intertwined in history. Then over there," he said, turning, "is the Garden of Gethsemane, sacred to Christians, and then here," he continued, "is the oldest Jewish cemetery in the world!"

Although there were people taking selfies on either side of us, I found the view of Jerusalem to be peaceful and magnificent.

After a few moments of silence, I asked them, "How is it for you to live here?" Khalil replied, "It is incredible and horrible," while Yara nodded in agreement. "It feels like we are double second-class citizens. Firstly, because we are Palestinians, and secondly, within the Palestinian community, we are considered second-class again because we are Christian."

Curious, I asked if they had ever considered emigrating. "We've discussed it many times," Khalil replied, "but the answer is 'no.' This place is our home; our family and roots are here. Although it often feels like the government is trying to make our lives so difficult that we will leave, we won't give up our home."

The first stars appeared over the city. Before leaving the area, Khalil asked, "Do you remember, Gio, that I told you that we will see sad and happy things?" I nodded. "One more sad thing, and then we will end with something happy."

We walked to the Garden of Gethsemane. When we arrived, it was empty, probably because it was already evening.

"We're standing at the place where Judas betrayed Christ," Yara said as we gazed at the ancient trees surrounding us. Khalil added, "During the destruction of Jerusalem, the Romans cut down all the trees around the city, so these olive trees might not be the same ones that witnessed the betrayal. However, olive trees are known to grow from saplings, meaning some plants here may have been present during that time. Regardless of the history, this is a special place," he concluded.

Though I didn't know many biblical stories by heart, the kiss of Judas was an exception. I imagined the crowd with torches entering the garden that night, waiting for Judas' signal: "The one I will kiss is the one. Arrest him." They might have come from the temple area we visited earlier or from the Praetorium and gathered stragglers and enemies along the way.

It was difficult for me to comprehend. The garden was serene and beautiful, and yet it was in that exact location where the ultimate betrayal took place. The name Judas has come to represent every act of betrayal since then. It was a terrible place, I thought to myself.

"Gio," Yara interrupted my thoughts. "This is where Jesus accepted his destiny. That's why I love it here."

Her words gradually changed my perspective, setting my mind at peace and making me feel grateful to be there with them.

"Come," Khalil said. "Now for joy."

We left and walked through the winding streets towards Khalil's house. When we turned onto their street, I heard music. Khalil and Yara exchanged glances and smiled. When we opened the door, they gestured for me to go first. Suddenly, there was a loud cry, "Surprise!" I turned around to see whose birthday it was. "Gio!" Yara said, "This is for you!" She laughed. "But it's not my birthday," I whispered. "We know that. It's not for your birthday. We are celebrating you."

A minute later, everyone was hugging and kissing. Khalil's father, Michel, pulled me aside and handed me a Taybeh beer. He clinked his bottle to mine and said, "We are so grateful you are here with us, Gio. Khalil loves you like a brother. You are family." He probably saw me blush as he pulled me towards him, kissed the top of my head, and led me back to the others.

"Gio, follow me!" Khalil said, starting to dance in moves that a Westerner like me would never be able to imitate. "Come on, Gio!" Yara said as she and others joined in. Soon, everyone, young, old, or in between, had their arms raised and hips swaying. So, I put my pride aside and let loose.

This was the joy that Khalil and Yara had promised.

Afterward, when I lay in bed that night, I felt so peaceful that I dozed off immediately.

We left for Bethlehem early the next day to explore the town before heading to Yara's family for lunch. Khalil drove since we had a lot of supplies to bring.

"Will there be any problems crossing into Palestinian territory?" I asked my friends.

"Not crossing over, but coming back, there can be issues. But don't worry, Gio, we have it all figured out," Yara said.

I was surprised that we arrived in Bethlehem in less than an hour.

The streets around the border crossing were chaotic: cars crowded the roads, with some double-parked and others triple-parked. Some honked and zipped around each other like acrobats. However,

# Onward

Khalil knew where to go and quickly found a great parking space outside the tourist zone.

As we walked over to Manger's Square, we passed by various businesses catering to tourists, such as souvenir shops, cafes, and hotels. I found the wood carving stores interesting, so we stopped by one of the shops to check out their olive wood statues and other figures. "Most of these wood shops are owned by Palestinian Christians, who rely on tourism. My brother, whom you will meet today, owns one," Yara informed me. "Maybe we can visit his shop later, but first, we are heading to the church of the Nativity, where Christ was born. Would you like to see it?" "For sure!" I replied with enthusiasm.

Yara made a phone call while we were walking, and I overheard her say, "We'll be there in five minutes." I asked her who she was talking to, and with a smile, she replied, "It was our priest, Father Elio. He will meet us there, show us around, and help us skip the line."

We saw him standing in the square in front of the ancient church. The priest was around my age, medium height and build, with black hair and a neatly trimmed goatee. Despite his Franciscan robe, he looked like he was from Hollywood with his sunglasses and haircut. As we approached, he exclaimed, "Buon giorno!" in Italian. Yara told him that I lived in Brindisi and introduced us. Father Elio warmly greeted us with a handshake and a hug. He then exclaimed, "You must be my brother from

Puglia! Taranto here, but now I live in Bethlehem. Welcome, welcome! Some here call me Elias, but I prefer Elio," he said.

It was a hot day, and the sun glared down on us already. Elio suggested that we take a moment in the shade before going inside. Once we found a spot, he asked Yara about her family. "They are doing well, but my mother wanted to invite you to lunch..." Elio started to refuse, but Yara interrupted, "She said not to take no for an answer and that if you declined, she wouldn't invite you again." There was a moment of silence, and then everyone burst out laughing. Yara rolled her eyes and said, "You know my mother." "OK," Elio replied. "I have a group coming at 1:30, so I can only stay for a few minutes." Yara nodded and said, "I'll call her now to let her know," as she stepped away.

Then Father Elio turned to me and asked, "Gio, why are you here? We are glad you are here, but why did you come to Bethlehem?" "For friendship." I responded, "Friendship is one of the most beautiful things humanity has ever come up with! I'm glad for you and happier for us," he said.

Elio seemed to have boundless energy, and I liked him. When Yara returned, he told us about the basilica's many secret passageways, hidden chapels, and centuries of spirituality. "When we enter," he said, "I'll ask you to refrain from talking until we stop. I want you to use all your senses to experience this place, letting it speak to you." We agreed.

# Onward

We stooped down to enter the "door of humility," an entrance from the Ottoman era that required us to bend low to get through. Elio later explained that it was designed to prevent attackers on horseback from entering.

We found ourselves in the nave and followed Elio's instructions to stay silent. He asked us to place our hands on one of the ancient columns lining both sides. Then, he invited us to look down at the floor, where some wood slabs had been removed, revealing a mosaic underneath. Elio encouraged us to look at the other mosaics from the middle of the nave. He whispered, "You have just seen the floor of Constantine's basilica underneath this one, which dates back to 326 AD. The columns you touched are also from that original building, holding up the nave today, which dates from the 6th century. There are multiple layers of history here. Now, look at those mosaics again and tell me what you see."

I looked up and saw many gold mosaic stones framing people, buildings, and plants. There were angels, apostles, and other holy individuals, but I couldn't understand what it all meant.

"Look, Gio," said Elio, noticing my perplexed expression. You can see Abraham, who represents the Old Testament covenant. Further down, you can see the kings of Israel wearing halos. This is all symbolic of Jesus' genealogy and shows the continuity between the Old and New Testaments. It represents the promise of salvation leading to its fulfillment.

"Now, take a closer look at the figures of Christ and Mary. The stories are told in terms of the fulfillment of prophecy. Christ represents the new ark of the covenant, the lamb's sacrifice, and the offering to the Father.

"Oh, and one more thing. Can you see which languages are written here?"

"I think it's in Latin and Greek," I responded. "Yes, Latin and Greek, east and west, the two lungs of the church. Unfortunately, they don't breathe together anymore, but it wasn't always like that," Elio explained.

Father Elio's enthusiasm for history and theology was evident. We stood silently for a moment before he said, "Come!"

We walked towards the altar area and then descended to the grotto of the Nativity. Elio spoke with the security guard, who allowed us to enter alone.

It was a small space with three altars, and beneath one was a 14-point silver star, indicating the traditional spot where Christ was born.

"Now, nobody knows for sure if this is the exact spot where Christ was born," Elio began, "but we celebrate his birth here. People have been coming here to honor his birth since the second century. St. Justin of Palestine, who died in 165, wrote that he knew the cave in Bethlehem where Jesus was born. Furthermore, the Romans built a temple to Adonis above this spot to quash Christian worship. So, the Roman Temple marked the spot. When Constantine's mother, Helen, came, she had the Temple dismantled and found this place where we are now standing."

After a brief pause, Elio said, "Come." We followed him through the church, past some chapels, through another corridor, and into another church. "This is the church of St. Catherine," he said, standing in the nave. "This is where I live." "You live in a church?" I blurted out. Yara and Elio chuckled. "Good question, Gio! I live in our monastery, which is attached to this church. I will show you. Come."

We followed him again, this time through a sunny cloister, and ended up in the monastery's kitchen. There was another Franciscan present there who was preparing lunch for the brothers. Elio introduced us: "These are my friends, Gio from Brindisi and Khalil and Yara from here," he said. After exchanging greetings, Elio asked Brother Filippo if there was any coffee. "Go sit in the refectory, and I will make you some," Filippo replied. Five minutes later, Filippo brought us three strong, steaming coffees and a plate of fresh rolls and placed them on the table. "Grazie amico," Elio thanked Filippo as he left.

As I looked around the dining hall, decorated with ancient frescoes and set with long tables for around twenty monks, I savored the moment while sipping my coffee. Father Elio surprised me when he asked, "Gio, what is your experience of the Holy Land so far?" I had to put down my drink and think before answering.

"It feels like I have walked into a big hug that keeps holding me close," I replied. Elio nodded and added, "Yes, she is a jealous lover, and once this land gets into your blood, she will always call you back." He then turned to Khalil and Yara and asked, "And what do you think?" Khalil responded, "I think life here is difficult, frustrating, wonderful, and beautiful. I wouldn't live anywhere else." Yara nodded in agreement.

When Yara looked at her watch, she jumped out of her seat. "My mother will not be happy if we are late!" she said. "Elio, will you stop by?" He nodded yes and said, "But only for a few minutes."

We thanked Elio for the fantastic morning and headed to Yara's house.

Yara's family owned an apartment on the outskirts of Bethlehem, where every building looked the same, with shops below and housing above. "Mama!" Yara called out as we entered her parents' modest home. Her mother rushed out of the kitchen with a strand of black hair on her face, a beaming smile, and dark, sparkling eyes. "My daughter!" she exclaimed and kissed Yara on both cheeks. "Gio, this is my mother, Anna." When I attempted to shake her hand, she also gave me kisses. "Gio, we're thrilled that you're here. Yara and Khalil can't stop talking about you. We're so delighted."

Yara looked around and asked, "Mama, where is everyone?" Anna smiled and replied, "They are upstairs. We reserved the rooftop terrace today.

Please go up; they are waiting for you. I am finishing here in the kitchen."

Yara insisted on helping her mother in the kitchen before heading upstairs.

As we climbed the three flights of stairs, Khalil explained, "Yara has three sisters and two brothers; all of them, along with her father, are here. A few family friends will join us, but most of our friends in Bethlehem have to work. Since tourism is the main industry, the shops and cafes must remain open when tourists are in town. Yara's family owns a souvenir shop near the church but closed it today. They wanted to celebrate."

As we stepped out onto the covered terrace, I was curious and started to ask, "Celebrate what?"

Arabic music was playing, and people were bustling about. Some were setting the table and arranging chairs, while others were organizing the food. Suddenly, one of Yara's sisters spotted us on the landing and called, "Papa!" A beefy, stout, gray-haired man rushed towards us and hugged me before embracing Khalil. "We are so happy you are here, Gio," he said. Then he hugged Khalil and added, "And you also, son." We were surrounded by sisters, brothers, cousins, and friends greeting us and asking about our morning, my background, and our plans.

"But you must see the shepherd's field," one said. "No, that's boring. We should take them to Nazareth; Gio will be amazed!" another said. The suggestions multiplied until Yara's father, Salim, raised his hands and said, "Children, give them some peace. Come, Gio and Khalil; sit with me in the shade and have something to drink."

The day was hot, but the beer was icy, and the atmosphere was lively.

Suddenly, someone cranked up the volume of the music, and everyone started dancing. "You boys, stay here," Salim said as he got up to assist his wife and Yara, who were climbing up the stairs. We trailed behind them, and I am glad we did. They carried tray after tray piled with cut veggies, hummus, fruits, cheese, and meats. How did she manage to fit all of that in her tiny kitchen?

With the table set, food served, and music lowered, Salim asked us to hold hands so he could pray. "Thank you for the food, Lord, the love and companionship you give us today. Especially thank you for Gio. He brings us much happiness. Amen."

I heard the exact phrase again, "Gio, we are so glad you are here," just like the previous evening. Did they think I was someone else? Maybe they thought I was someone famous?

I had imposter syndrome again, but I managed to overcome it with the help of Khalil, Yara, and a few beers.

"Gio, do you think Yara shouldn't color her hair blonde?" Anna, Yara's mother, asked while sitting next to me. Before I could respond, Yara said, "Mama, you know it helps us not to get stopped at the checkpoint!" Confused, I turned to Yara and asked, "What?"

"When we return to Jerusalem," Yara began, "we have to go through the Israeli checkpoint. The soldiers use racial profiling to stop certain cars and can delay you for hours while they search your car, look at your papers, and just harass you. The more non-Arab you look, the less chance they will stop you. For example, they haven't stopped me once since I dyed my hair blond. It used to happen all the time."

I must have had a shocked expression because Yara kept on speaking.

"When Khalil and I drive together, he puts in an earring; the soldiers don't think Arab men are cool enough to have body piercings. Tattoos are also a way to slide through a checkpoint; my sister, when visiting me, puts a henna tattoo on her arm and ensures the soldiers see it. They don't think Palestinians would have a tattoo. Another tactic is music; we never play Arabic music near a checkpoint, but no music can arouse suspicion. A few days ago, my sister zipped right through the checkpoint with her tattoo on her arm and Madonna blasting on the radio. Another thing that helps is washing the car before the checkpoint since the soldiers think we all have dirty cars. Oh, and one more thing; they think all Palestinians are homophobic, so a gay pride sticker guarantees not to get stopped."

"Let the boy eat, Yara!" Anna scolded her daughter. Yara rolled her eyes, smiled, and took another helping of food. "She eats like she's storing food in her legs, like a camel," Khalil teased her.

I don't recall all the conversations from that afternoon around the table, but I remember plenty of platters being passed, glasses being filled, conversations shifting, and lots of laughter.

As Anna started serving dessert and coffee, Father Elio arrived. Everyone stood up to greet him as Anna tried to hand him a plate full of cakes. He politely refused the offer of sweets. "No sweets for me, Anna; I need to keep fit so I can be around a long time," he said. Although Anna insisted, he gracefully stood his ground. I admired his passion and focus on how he wanted to live.

As the sun set, we had to prepare to return to Jerusalem. Anna and Salim asked us to stay longer and even offered us a place to sleep. However, Yara and Khalil had plans for us in Jerusalem. Yara thanked her parents and kissed them.

"Gio, when will you visit us again?" Anna turned towards me and asked. I stuttered for a moment, saying that I wasn't sure, but hopefully soon. "Please come again; we'll miss you," she said, with Salim nodding in agreement.

Elio had to leave, too, so after several hugs and kisses, the four of us departed. Elio walked us to our car and said, "Gio, sometimes I go to Taranto to visit my family. If you're in Brindisi, let's meet up! You can take me on your sailing boat, and I'll take you on my

father's fishing boat. We'll see which one is better."
We agreed.

After saying goodbye to us, Elio hugged me and
advised me, "Remember the jealous lover, and when
she calls you back, don't resist. We will all be here
waiting for you." As we drove off, Elio stayed on the
street, waving goodbye.

Blond Yara was driving with ear-ringed Khalil
sitting beside her, and I was in the back of the car as
we listened to Metallica blasting from the stereo.
When we approached the checkpoint, the soldiers
waved us through, and we made it to Khalil's house
in record time.

Upon our return, we were tired and decided to
have a simple dinner with Khalil's family. We went
to bed early; my last day in Jerusalem would be the
following.

The following day, I woke up to the aroma of
brewing coffee. As I stumbled downstairs, I found
Khalil helping his mother, Mariana, set out breakfast,
including flatbread, hummus, boiled eggs, olives,
freshly sliced tomatoes, and cucumbers. "Coffee,
please," I managed to say. Since the light coming
through the window was too bright and I was
squinting, I didn't notice Yara sitting in the corner
until she laughed. "Good morning, Gio," greeted
Khalil's mother, Mariana. I apologized and said, "Oh,
sorry, good morning. Coffee, please." Mariana
laughed, then handed me a steaming cup of coffee.

"Someone is not a morning person," Yara teased. "Usually, I am, but not today," I replied.

After the coffee started to kick in, I greeted Mariana again and thanked her for the spread. We then discussed our plans for the day. Mariana suggested doing something fun as considered different activities. "Maybe Gio needs a break from all the history and politics here," she added. Yara asked me, "What do you think, Gio?" I replied, "Fun sounds great to me." The three of us brainstormed ideas for a minute and came up with a plan. "Let's do the Ramparts Walk; we'll walk along the old city wall to Damascus gate, and whenever we come across something interesting, we can explore it." We raised our coffee cups in agreement.

Before heading out, Mariana reminded us to return home for dinner. "This is Gio's last day, so we want it to be special," she said.

We decided to hike the rampart walls' northern and southern sections, which would take about three hours, starting at Jaffa gate. We paid our fee, ascended the stairs, and started our trek around the city.

During our walk around Jerusalem, we visited the Muslim, Christian, Armenian, and Jewish quarters, which helped me understand the city's layout. We passed old churches, mosques, synagogues, modern parking lots, and rundown neighborhoods. We saw locals and tourists and enjoyed stunning views of the city's historical monuments and panoramic landscapes. However, the residential areas outside the old city were not pretty. Overall, it was a remarkable journey through the ancient and modern parts.

After a few hours, my stomach began to grumble.

"I'm hungry too," Yara said, laughing after hearing my grumbles. So, we abandoned our rampart adventure and headed towards the Mahane Yehuda Market.

The market had around 250 vendors, and we spent the rest of the day there. We purchased enough food to feed a family of ten, including kibbeh, kebab, and kanafeh.

Afterward, we found a patch of grass outside the market area where we could relax and eat.

While devouring my kebab, I exclaimed, "This is incredible!" Yara added, "I could eat here all day." Khalil joked, "Don't tell my mother!" We all laughed.

To our surprise, we consumed all the food and drank three large bottles of cold sparkling water.

While sitting on the grass, I was the first to lay back, followed by Khalil and Yara. The sky was a deep blue with wisps of clouds crossing the summer sky. Khalil put a blade of grass between his teeth and grew reflective.

"Gio, how do you feel about leaving tomorrow?" he asked. I had so many emotions in the past few days that it took me a minute to sort them out.

"I feel happy about our friendship and grateful for your families, but I also feel a little sad," I admitted.

"We are sad too, Gio!" Yara began. "Why don't you stay longer?" she said, sitting up.

I shook my head regretfully. "I wish I could."

"When will you return?" Khalil asked.

"I don't know yet, my friend," I replied. "Tomorrow, I will leave for Tel Aviv in the morning. I need to get some supplies and prepare the boat for the long sail back to Brindisi. But..." I paused as an idea came to me that began to germinate.

"But, why don't you come with me? Hear me out," I said as I sat up. "We could take the train early in the morning and sail along the coast. I can get my supplies later, even in the evening. Then you can hop on the train and return here tomorrow evening! It's just one day!"

The two looked at each other, so I pushed the issue.

"You only live once! Come, let's do it!" I almost pleaded.

"I think that would be wonderful, an experience I would never forget, no Yara? But there are two challenges. The first is work. Yara, can you get tomorrow off?" he asked. She put her hand on her stomach. "Suddenly, I have a stomach ache; my boss will understand that food poisoning has to be taken seriously." We laughed, and then Yara added, "But what about you, Khalil? You know you are expected in the office tomorrow." He then grabbed his stomach as if he had a sudden cramp. "Oh, your stomach ache is contagious! I think I can't go to work tomorrow either!"

We high-fived each other, but Khalil mentioned that there was still one more challenge. "My mother. She will worry if I tell her we are going sailing. She would be happy if we told her we would go to Tel Aviv with you to help you with your boat. And that isn't a lie, is it, Gio? We will help you sail your boat."

We were all excited about spending the next day on the water. "Khalil, your mother is probably planning a big dinner later. Why don't we go home and rest? I need a nap," I suggested. Half an hour later, we were each in our respective rooms. I smiled as I lay down, feeling happy.

My phone rang, and it was Matteo. "Have you been converted yet?" he teased. "I am probably as converted as you," I responded. "Well," he replied, "You know me, Gio. Always one foot in and one out. Except when it comes to my wife; with her, it is both feet in, but not only feet," he said, chuckling. "Stop! Too much information," I shot back. We then updated each other about the events of the past days, including Khalil and Yara's family's welcome. "But I'm your family," Matteo responded. "Yes, brother, you are; nothing will change that. But our family may get a little bigger; it doesn't change who you are for me." Matteo paused, then added, "Gio, I have some news. I am not supposed to tell anyone yet, but I will share it with you. Our family is about to get bigger on my side. Chiara just found out she is pregnant; we will have a baby, Gio! Can you believe that?" "Wow, my brother Matteo is becoming a father! How do you feel about that?" Matteo sighed. "I am happy, worried, grateful, fearful, hopeful, and humbled, if that makes any sense. I feel like I finally have to grow up, my friend. As you are growing up, passing from Tel Aviv to Jerusalem…"

Matteo's final words stuck with me as I dozed off.

We all slept until dinner when Khalil woke me up by knocking on my door. Heading downstairs, we found a table set for about fifteen relatives and friends of the family. Thankfully, it wasn't a party but a family dinner that Anna had organized. I was relieved not to be the center of attention.

Michel called out to Khalil and me and asked us to come over to the other side of the room. He put his arm over Khalil's shoulders and the other over mine, saying, "I am so happy you are here. And I am proud of both of you."

He then turned to me and added, "Gio, we are sad you are leaving tomorrow, but we know you will be back." I thanked him but still wondered what he saw in me that I did not see in myself.

The dinner was a comfortable gathering for the whole family. Everyone was chatting, complimenting the food, sharing their day, and telling stories. I felt at ease, content, and peaceful, like a brother among his siblings.

# Onward

After dessert, Khalil whispered, "Gio, mamma, and papa want to talk to you in the next room." When I asked him why, he just shrugged.

Michel invited everyone to stay at the table and play music while coffee was brewing.

Michel then took me into his study and closed the door, where Marianna was waiting. I wondered if I had done something wrong.

The two invited me to sit while they sat in front of me. They briefly spoke to each other in Arabic, and there was some awkwardness.

Then Marianna began.

"Gio, when Khalil told me about your parents, I cried. It's hard to imagine what it must have felt like to suddenly find yourself without a family, barely knowing how to face the world alone. But look at what you have accomplished with your life!" Then Michel continued, "Others, with less heart, might have given up or let that loss weigh them down. But that's not you. We are proud of you and happy you are part of Khalil and Yara's lives." Then Marianna continued, "We are so happy you have come into our lives, Gio. We wish that you didn't have to leave."

I thought they were leading up to something but couldn't quite get there.

They glanced at each other, and then Michel continued.

"Gio," he said, "we would be so happy if you could visit us during Christmas. You can stay with us anytime you want; you always have your same room here. So, firstly, we want to say that you are welcome here! Secondly," he continued as he pulled out his wallet, "we want to buy your plane ticket for you." As he spoke, he started taking out hundred-dollar bills.

I begged, "No, no, no, please stop." Then, I made a quick decision. "Yes, I will come during Christmas, but only on one condition." Both of them looked at me expectantly. "My condition is that I will buy my own ticket." When they started to protest, I added, "Otherwise, I won't come."

They agreed, and both hugged me before joining the others.

"Gio is going to visit us during Christmas!" they announced. Everyone cheered and clapped.

When I sat down, Khalil said, "I told Youseff about tomorrow, Gio, and now he is begging to come. Is that OK?"

"Sure, that's fine," I replied. "But you'll have to explain to your parents tomorrow. I don't want to lie to them."

The next morning, we headed downstairs for breakfast. Michel and Marianna were already in the kitchen, chatting in Arabic and sipping coffee. When we entered, they put down their cups and hugged us warmly. Marianna poured each of us a cup of coffee and brought plates of warm flatbread, hummus, cucumbers, and eggs.

Then, she went to the pantry and brought out a big box. "This is for your trip," she announced. "Just a little something to keep you from getting hungry today."

"Mama!" Youseff groaned.

Marianna just smiled. "It's nothing much," she said.

Strong emotions filled the room, and as we stood to say our goodbyes, Marianna and Michel were in tears. "Remember our agreement, son," Michel said, wiping his eyes as we departed.

Less than three hours later, we were on my boat in Tel Aviv. It was hard to comprehend the two worlds I had experienced in just one week.

The day was sunny and beautiful as we sailed up the coast, passing by some of the same sites I had seen with Sofia and Sebastian, but today felt different. I had a sense of belonging with Youseff, Yara, and Khalil, which changed my experience. We spent the day chatting, laughing, telling stories, and enjoying Anna's food. I hadn't felt so happy in a long time.

As the evening approached, my friends and I returned to the marina in Tel Aviv. They helped me to purchase and carry supplies for the next day's return journey. When we said goodbye, there was no sadness as we knew our bond would endure time and distance.

My return sail followed the same plan as my arrival. I stopped at Cyprus, Rhodes, and the Greek mainland before heading to Italy. I planned to spend a night at each place, gather supplies, and, depending on the winds, arrive back in Brindisi the following week.

The next day, the winds were favorable, and at dawn, I set out, marveling at the orange and red hues of the sky that transformed it into an impressionist painting. As I moved towards Cyprus, I couldn't help but think of Noam and Khalil, Sofia and Yara, and Sebastian and Elio. They lived in different worlds, yet I was a part of both.

I realized that I had outgrown Tel Aviv and that my path lay somewhere between Jerusalem and Bethlehem.

# Chapter 12
# Death and Gratitude in Algeria

"**P**lease, Gio, do not do this. Please reconsider," was the first message I received from a friend when I told them about my plan to sail to Algeria. Another friend, Matteo, called me and said, "Gio, this is Matteo again. Remember what I said, don't do it." Over the next few days, Pierre in France, Sadiki in Egypt, and even Samuru in Barcelona called me to convince me not to go. Masika was the only person who supported my idea, but that was because she wanted to come along. "If you bring Masika, I will divorce you and her!" Sadiki said a few days later, and we both laughed.

I had never visited Algeria before, and I didn't have any local connections there. Although I appreciate my friendships, I wanted to explore beyond the usual places where I had friends. Even though there is a big difference between not knowing any locals and landing on the Côte d'Azur and the coast of Algeria, I wanted to experience the Sahara since life is short. Despite the warnings and concerns of my friends, I was determined to go.

I read about the government's warnings regarding terrorism and kidnappings in the country. However, I also read about the safer areas and the precautions that can be taken for a fantastic adventure. Other people had traveled to Algeria safely, so why couldn't I?

My friends were persistent and would drive me crazy unless I agreed to some of their terms. These included keeping Matteo as my primary contact and checking in with him daily, avoiding the border areas, staying away from public tourist areas with crowds, triple-checking the background of a guide before hiring him, not dressing like an American, and not taking any chances.

I agreed to all the conditions because I was aware of the risks of heading into an area I knew little about. Furthermore, I knew this would be a challenging sail, so I planned to break it up by stopping in Sicily for a few days and then on to Tunisia for a rest. From there, I would head to Algiers, where a harbor in Sidi Fredj is a safe tourist area, where I would make my base.

I decided to focus on Southern Algeria for my desert trek due to its incredible vistas, intriguing villages, and ancient cave paintings. In the weeks leading up to my trip, I researched the area and organized all my papers and passport. However, I still needed to find a reliable guide and a car for the journey, which I planned to do once I arrived.

# Onward

Despite my eagerness to get started, it took me about a week to reach my destination due to my sailing route. But finally, I landed in Southern Algeria, ready to begin my adventure.

Amir was the manager of the marina at Sidi Fredj. When I arrived and went through immigration, I introduced myself and shook his hand, hoping to establish a good rapport. From my travels, I learned that forming relationships was essential in making a journey transformative. Although Amir spoke some English, he was more comfortable speaking in French, which was fine for me. Sometimes, I accidentally spoke in Italian, but my French was good enough to get by. "Please come in and have some tea, Monsieur Jovanny," he invited me, pointing towards his cluttered office.

I explained my goals to Amir: adventure, independence, safety, and the ability to keep my friends posted. Amir, a large man with a dark, bushy beard, thick hair, and big black eyes, thoughtfully considered my words as he leaned back in his chair. "Monsieur Jovanny," he began, leaning forward, "you have two options. Firstly, you can travel with a group organized by an agency. This way, you'll experience the Sahara safely but lose some of your independence. Secondly, you can travel with a guide. This way, you'll keep your independence but sacrifice some of your safety. When I say 'safety,' I am not referring to violence or kidnapping, but things like your vehicle breaking down or an injury. We don't take visitors into areas where there is unrest. So, you can choose to go with a group or a guide. These are your options."

"I'm not a fan of traveling with a group since it takes away from the experience," I told Amir. "However, I'm unsure if traveling alone with just a guide is safe. I should gain some experience here first to make a better decision."

Amir had a suggestion. "Why don't you try talking to other tourists in town? They can share their experiences and help you find the best tours, agencies, or guides. You can even speak to my son, who is also a guide. Take a few days to research and plan the experience you want in the Sahara."

I agreed to Amir's suggestion and headed towards the town center, where I spotted a café where many tourists with pale skin, western clothes, and wide-brim hats were gathered. I ordered a cold mint tea and sat at a nearby table, listening in on conversations of couples and groups.

"I can't stand it; it's so dirty! Mom, I want to go home!" I overheard an American teenage girl complain to her parents while sitting at the table next to mine. "Shut up, Kaley!" her brother snapped back. The negative energy at that table made me turn my attention elsewhere.

I noticed a group of six or seven people sitting behind me. Some were British, while others were American. The Americans were the loudest ones in the group. However, I started paying attention when

I heard one of them say, "Our guide was fantastic! Even though it wasn't on the itinerary, he changed our schedule when we told him we wanted to see more cave paintings. And the food he and his crew came up with! They turned charred wood into an oven to bake bread! I would definitely use them again."

I turned around, introduced myself to the group, and said, "Hello, my name is Jovanny. I just arrived and want to join a group or hire a guide. I overheard you talking about your experience with your guide, and I was wondering if you could tell me more about it. Maybe I'll consider going with them."

My question was all they needed. The Americans began talking over each other and soon were joined by the Brits, each sharing their experiences of their time in the Sahara. They gave me the name of the tour company and their guide. I thanked them, paid my bill, and returned to the marina.

I wanted to avoid traveling with a group as it wasn't my usual way of exploring new places. However, I also wanted to avoid getting stranded in the Sahara desert without water and dying. When I arrived at the port, I was looking for a middle ground and had a proposal to make to Amir.

"I would like to hire your son as my guide to explore the desert, but I also want to travel with a group. We can participate in some of the group visits but also have the option of going off on our own. We will always begin and end our days with the group without being bound by their schedule. My cover story will be that I am researching a book about Algeria," I explained to Amir. He looked skeptical but listened attentively.

Amir scratched his head and replied, "This seems very complicated. Moreover, it would be more expensive since you will pay for two guides. Do you have any specific guide or tour company in mind?" I mentioned the names suggested by other travelers in the town. Amir smiled and said, "I know this company; we have worked together before. Also, the guide is my son's friend; they have led groups into the desert together. If he leads the group and my son accompanies you as your personal guide, it could work out well. Why don't you give me a day or two to arrange everything?

"Meanwhile, explore the city and enjoy the sights. I will see what we can do for you."

We shook hands, and I left.

I wasn't sure if I was being taken advantage of, but my gut told me I could trust Amir. However, my gut was sometimes wrong.

The following day, Amir called me and apologized for interrupting my sightseeing. "Come, meet my son Sami this afternoon. He will be your guide; your journey into the Sahara begins tomorrow. Sami has already made arrangements with the tour operator. He will bring you to their office so you can make payment and any other arrangements," he said.

At the time of the call, I was lying on the beach. I asked Amir if we could meet at 2 o'clock, which would give me enough time to enjoy the water for a few hours. Amir agreed, and we hung up after confirming the time.

I went straight from the beach to meet Sami, a young man about 25 years old who was thin and energetic, with long black hair in a ponytail and intense eyes. He greeted me in accented English and suggested we go to a cafe to discuss the trip's logistics. But first, I asked Sami to accompany me to Amir's office.

"I have some friends who want to keep in touch with me while I am here. How does that work out in the desert?" I asked. Amir laughed and said, "It doesn't! There is no phone service away from the towns. But do not worry, my friend. Sami can get me a message if he needs to. Give your friends my phone number; they can call me for information. But tell them not to worry! Algeria is safe!"

I gave Amir's phone number to Matteo and assured him that everything would be alright, asking him to stop worrying. Afterward, I met with Sami to discuss our upcoming trip, meet the other guide, and purchase the necessary supplies.

Sami said, "The most important thing is not to get lost in the desert, so please don't wander off alone. The second thing to remember is to ensure we don't end up with two groups. If anyone in the group asks to come with us on a day excursion, we will always say no. We will always say that you are doing secret research." That was perfectly fine with me; I wanted the luxury of group travel without additional responsibilities.

I arrived early at our meeting point at dawn the following day. Three airport transfer vehicles were waiting in the tour agency's parking lot. Sami and the other guide were smoking and watching coffee brewing on a small stove on the ground. "Jovanny!" Sami called out, handing me a small cup of the concentrated brew. "I put the sugar in for you," he said. I sipped the intense, overly-sweetened coffee in the crisp dawn air.

"Hello! Good morning!" a middle-aged American couple shouted while dragging their suitcase. Soon, the rest of the group arrived. "How many?" I whispered to Sami. "Thirteen in the group and us," he said, pointing to himself, the other guide, and me. "Sixteen people in total," he added. I thought it could be worse.

To save time, we would fly to Djanet. From there, we would venture into the Sahara in southern Algeria, which was said to be the most spectacular area.

As we drove to the airport, checked in our bags, and boarded the plane, I felt exhausted and barely conscious. I must have dozed off during the flight because the next thing I knew, Sami shook me and said, "Jovanny, we're here! We've arrived in Djanet!"

We quickly exited the airport and found our transportation waiting outside. I dozed off again in the jeep, and when I woke up, we were off-road in the middle of the desert.

Our adventure began at Tassili n'Ajjer National Park. We drove across the sand to the plateau, and countless giant rock formations surrounded the area. When the jeeps stopped, we got out, and I turned in a circle to see the vastness of the Sahara, which made me feel small, like a grain of sand. While our guide gave us a history and geology lesson, two teenagers in the group took out their drones. I looked at Sami, and he nodded. After whispering to the other guide, we left the group to embark on our adventure.

We got into Sami's jeep, drove for about half an hour, parked, and then hiked until we reached a massive rock formation that towered over the surroundings.

We walked part way around a rock mound and eventually found ourselves standing in front of a detailed carving depicting some animals that appeared to be drinking. Upon closer inspection, I noticed that the animals had tears running down their faces. "It is called the Weeping Cows," Sami whispered. He paused to let me take it in. He then slowly began to tell me the story of the carving.

"An ancient shepherd and his herd once got lost in this desert. They were thirsty and had run out of water. The shepherd saw water on the horizon, right where we are now. He led his cattle across the desert, taking days to reach this spot. But when they arrived, they discovered it was just a mirage and no water. The cattle were devastated and began to weep. One by one, they died of thirst. With his remaining strength, the shepherd carved these images so that his story would not be lost."

"How sad," I said, looking closer. "But look," Sami continued, "water gathers here when it rains," he pointed to an indentation at the base of the carvings. "And the shepherd was such a fine artist that you can see the crying cows bowing down to drink from it for all eternity when there is rain. So that is their reward. They died on this spot, but they live forever in the minds of visitors like you and me, and when there is rain, they drink."

"But it never rains here," I objected. "These lands were very different when these paintings were created, Monsieur Jovanny. I will show you other figures of hippopotami and other water-loving creatures in this area. The climate has evolved from their time to ours, and the desert has expanded. So we can see a window into the past when rain in this spot was not so rare."

"But if this story is true, and that is a big 'but,'" I began, "why would someone dying of thirst take the time to make this carving? Why not just escape and leave the herd behind?" Sami laughed and replied, "I can see that you do not know shepherds. They would never abandon their herd; their herd is part of them; it is their life. Perhaps he knew he would die and realized that this was his only chance to live forever."

The theme of wanting to live forever had followed me from Egypt.

"Come," said Sami as we walked back to our jeep.

We spent the rest of the afternoon driving and hiking around Tassili n'Ajjer, searching for prehistoric rock paintings.

Sami took me to a well-known cave, which was dark, cool, and empty of tourists. After we entered, he pointed towards the figures of men and animals running on the stone above our heads. He then told me, "Imagine that what you see here is like a photograph of the past. You see men and animals running, chasing, pursuing, and being chased; this was life before men knew how to farm or herd. Look into the past here, Monsieur Jovanny. Can you see?"

The images were simple but captured the essence of each person and animal. Most animals depicted on those rock walls no longer exist in this area. They have either become extinct or pushed out by the changing climate.

While I was lost in thought, Sami laid a blanket on the ground and said, "Come, lie here and look up. I will give you some time to contemplate the past, the origins from which we all come." Then he disappeared.

The ancient mural felt like a telescope, allowing a view of events from tens of thousands of years ago. It depicted warriors with bows and arrows on one side and human figures herding giant-horned steers on the other. It felt like a transitional point between a life based on hunting and one based on herding. Witnessing this change from surviving in the wild to taming it was remarkable.

The communities that herded animals could now settle in one place, build towns, and eventually cities. As I gazed at this mural, I felt like I was witnessing humanity take a huge step forward.

"Are you ready, Monsieur Jovanny?" whispered Sami. Before I could get up, he knelt beside me and looked up. "What did you see?" he asked.

I paused to reflect. "I saw men realize that they were not just other beasts. They are beginning to see that there is more to life than just chasing after food."

"Good man!" Sami said. "Then you are ready to see our next wonder, but that will be tomorrow. Now, we must return to camp."

The other travelers were curious about how we had spent our day; my responses were friendly but vague. Sami explained, "Monsieur Jovanny is doing important research for his book," which generated more questions. "I really can't share specific details until I complete the research phase," I said, ending the discussion.

Early the following day, we all traveled to Tamrit and worked together to set up our base camp. We planned to explore the Cypress Valley of Tamrit and the Big Canyon.

After finishing setting up the group's tents, Sami whispered that he had a plan. "Today, we will take it easy and see some of the scenery and paintings in the area. However, tomorrow, we will hike to Sefar. I will show you something I cannot describe," he said. I asked why we couldn't go right now. He replied, "It is a four-hour hike, and we must start early." I put my trust in Sami's hands.

Seeing trees in the Sahara seemed both odd and refreshing. Tamrit's Cypress Valley is a remnant of a wetter climate when forests covered the area. My guide informed me that some cypresses were thousands of years old. "The desert is not dead," Sami said. "One just needs to know where to look."

I was grateful for this calmer day, as the following would require almost all of my strength.

"We are going back in time today, back over 10,000 years, Monsieur Jovanny," Sami said the following day as we set out. It was hours before dawn, so we crept silently to avoid waking anyone. Sami had packed food and water for the journey. "I will make coffee and breakfast in an hour," he whispered as we hiked on the sand and between rock formations that seemed to be from another planet.

True to his word, we stopped an hour later. Sami took out his portable stove and had coffee brewing in ten minutes. We both sat on a rock and gazed at the stars while sipping our coffee and eating the bread and cheese he had packed. We were quiet as we looked at the vast expanse above and around us.

We continued our hike and arrived at our destination about three and a half hours later. I still didn't know what he wanted to show me. He instructed me to follow him and observe without judgment. "No tourists are here. I will lead you in; look, but do not judge. See how it speaks to you," he said. We entered the cave and stood before a series of rock paintings. The largest painting was about four meters tall and depicted a towering figure rising above images of animals and humans. On one side of the painting was a group of women kneeling before the central figure. At first glance, the central figure appeared to be a monster, with its human body, strange bumps on its biceps, and a head that looked like horns were coming out from everywhere.

"It looks like a scary monster," I said to Sami, who laughed. He then put one hand on my shoulder, guiding my gaze with the other. "When you look at this figure compared to the others, what is the first thing you see?" he asked. "It's huge!" I said. "Yes, it is enormous. Its size means greatness. This painting depicts something great. Now, look at the arms; what do you see?" "Weird bumps," I said. Sami laughed again and pointed. "Monsieur Jovanny, what do big biceps mean?" I thought for a minute and saw where he was going. "Strength," I said. "Yes, yes!" he replied excitedly. "Now," he continued, pointing, "what do you notice about the head?" I shook my head as I looked. "It doesn't look human." Sami nodded. "Yes, but then what is it?" he insisted. "I can't tell. It is strange; it's some mysterious creature I've never seen," I replied. "Mysterious! Yes, Monsieur Jovanny, mysterious! The shape of the head means that this being is mysterious. Now, you can see the meaning of the painting. He is great, strong, and mysterious! Do you see now?" he asked. I looked at the figure again, and it became clear that the human figures on one side were paying homage to it. "It must be a god," I said. "Yes," Sami replied, "the god of Sefar."

I looked at the figures scattered across the wall – drawings of animals and humans going about their daily lives, with a strange creature looming above them. "What do you think?" Sami asked.

"I wonder why they needed to believe in a powerful god. Perhaps they felt threatened..." I began, but Sami interrupted me.

"No, my friend, you are going down the wrong path. You Westerners think of belief as a weakness. You think those who are afraid, ignorant of science, or don't know any better develop a belief in one greater than themselves. If you come here with that mindset, you will never understand what you see!"

Sami turned to me with an intense expression, but I didn't understand what he was trying to say. "What's the alternative?" I asked, trying to see his point.

"These people, 10,000 years ago, didn't make this figure because they were afraid or ignorant! Many tourists believe this, but it isn't true."

"So why did they paint it?" I asked.

Sami struggled to find the right words. He turned to face the figure again and began speaking.

"Many people go through life asking only 'how' questions. Questions like 'How do I get food?', or 'How do I get a better job?', ' How can I support a family?' or 'How can I buy a car?' These are all questions about survival. But in this cave, the ancient humans asked a different question: 'Why?' They asked, 'Why am I here? What is my purpose?' These are not weak or ignorant questions but rather questions that show our humanity. To be alive is not just about survival but also about finding meaning in life. When I begin to ask these questions, I can understand the belief in the god of Sefar."

Sami grew silent as we continued to look at the images.

When I glanced over at him, I saw that he had tears in his eyes. He turned and walked outside.

I gave him a few minutes to gather himself. Sami's ability to reflect on life and the meaning of the stone paintings was remarkable. Something about the history and spirit of these images lived inside him.

We hiked back to camp in silence.

Our group journeyed deeper into the desert towards Tin Merzouga the following day. As we drove, the color of the sand changed from yellow to orange and then to red. It was a land of enormous, eerie rock formations and dunes as giant as warehouses. The group had planned to explore the rocks on the first day and the dunes on the second. So, Sami and I decided to do the opposite.

As the sunset approached, we arrived at our campsite. After consulting with the other guide, Sami asked me to join him in climbing one of the highest dunes. "Monsieur Jovanny, please climb this dune. See what the desert speaks to you. Watch the sunset. Then come down to the camp, where we will set up dinner. Please do not miss this opportunity."

I didn't mean much encouragement. Sami handed me a water bottle, and I was off, trekking up the sandy slope.

I felt smaller and smaller as I climbed higher. Words can't describe the feeling better than "small." It was like I was shrinking in an endless ocean of dunes. The landscape was all red waves with rocky outcroppings that dotted the area with shadows. The colors were burning orange and red from the sun, and the dunes seemed to grow around me. It was like I was an ant of a man, getting smaller with every step and disappearing into insignificance before the vast backdrop of the Sahara.

I finally understood what Sami meant by "let the desert speak." I sat at the dune's ridge as the sun dipped behind the sandy horizon.

I knew our camp was nearby, but I neither saw nor heard nor sensed any human presence. I felt aloneness and smallness so thick that I could almost slice it, but it wasn't a sad feeling. The realization that beauty was immense and I was small filled me with an emotion that I couldn't quite put my finger on.

Like the massive god at Sefar, I was before something greater that I couldn't define, capture, or enclose. Somehow, it embraced me.

"Monsieur Jovanny!!!" Sami called from below. I looked up at the first stars appearing and smiled. "Thank you," I whispered to the Sahara before descending to the camp.

"Has the desert spoken to you?" Sami asked as I reached the camp. "Oh yes, she spoke," I replied. He smiled as if he understood.

We spent a few more days exploring the Sahara, but none was as powerful as my encounter with the god of Sefar and the voice of the desert at sunset at the pinnacle of that dune.

It was time for me to return home. So, we packed up our things, drove for what seemed like forever, took a flight, and drove again. Once we arrived in Sidi Fredj, I longed to be back among the dunes and rock paintings. The noise and chaos of the town made my head hurt, and I wanted to escape.

"Hey, Sami," I asked. "Can you help me get a car for a few days?" Sami looked at me skeptically. "What do you have planned?" he asked. "I just want to explore the area and get away from here until it's time to leave." Sami looked into my eyes. "Sure, I can help you get a car for a few days, but promise me that you will be careful. Do not go further than a hundred kilometers from the town; do not stop in isolated areas. Do you promise?" I agreed.

# Onward

Somehow, the desert experience had changed me. I felt a great sense of peace and a longing for more than the town's confines could offer. Not even my boat was drawing me; something about unending red dunes rolling towards the horizon had expanded my spirit.

Sami got me an old rental car from a buddy of his. "Sorry, Jovanny, this is all I could find at the last moment," he said. The car was fine; I just needed to escape.

I jumped in and headed towards the horizon. "Do not go beyond one hundred kilometers," Sami had urged me, "and come back tonight; do not sleep out in unfamiliar areas." I promised Sami I would return that evening but secretly decided to drive further than a hundred kilometers.

The drive helped me clear my head and ease back into my world from the one I had been in. When the stars started to come out, I turned around and headed back to town.

The moonlight reflecting on the landscape was beautiful, and a few days of exploring the area alone was the perfect way to conclude my trip.

However, my peaceful drive back to town was interrupted when I saw a small group gathered on the side of the isolated road. As I got closer, I noticed a crushed bicycle lying on its side and what appeared to be a body lying on the ground beside it. One of the bystanders tried to flag me down, but I hesitated, recalling Sami's warnings about such situations.

When I drove past them, one of the men took pictures of my car with his phone.

What was going on, I wondered. Should I call the police or emergency services? As I reached for my phone to call Sami, I realized I was out of signal range.

After a long time without any signal, I finally got in range and saw that Sami had called three times, Amir had called four times, and even Matteo had called twice from Brindisi. It seemed like something terrible had happened. I checked my text messages, and several said, "Call Amir as soon as you get this."

As my heart raced, I dialed Amir's number, and he picked up on the first ring. "Jovanny, where are you?" I estimated that I was around thirty minutes away from the marina and told him so. "Head straight to the marina right now. Don't stop for anyone; try not to draw any attention to yourself, and please take off that baseball hat! You could be in danger. I'll explain everything when you get here. Please don't ask any questions now. HURRY!"

I called Matteo and asked what was going on. "My friend, we have been so worried! Amir called me because he could not reach you. Have you spoken with him? Yes, you must have. He told me that your car was at the scene of an accident. The police are searching for you; Amir said it is for questioning since someone claimed that you caused the death of someone on a bicycle. Amir said you could be arrested even if the accusation is false because someone may be looking for a bribe; they could detain you until you pay. Gio, you must leave Algeria tonight. Please call me when you are on your boat."

I pushed on the gas of my rental wreck and made it to the marina in record time. Amir and Sami were waiting for me outside. They quickly took my bag from the trunk, and Sami drove the car away. Meanwhile, Amir led me towards my boat. "I am sorry for this conclusion to your trip, Monsieur Jovanny, but your safety comes first."

I unlatched the boat, started the engine, and was off in ten minutes. I could unfurl the sails later.

My heart was beating so fast, and everything seemed so surreal. It took me a few hours at sea to understand what had happened.

I sent messages to Amir and Sami to express my gratitude. Then, I used my VHF radio to call Matteo. "We are all waiting to hear from you! Are you alright, Gio?" "Yes, my friend, I am on my way home."

"I am so relieved; you cause your friends a lot of stress!" he said and laughed. "So tell me, was it worth it?"

I told him about the ancient rock paintings, the never-ending waves of dunes, the rock formations that looked like cities, and the traces of a flourishing land filled with giraffes and hippopotami which has now disappeared. I continued recounting the feelings I had while watching the sunset over the Sahara and the confusion I experienced when I drove past a corpse on the side of the road, followed by the fear of being arrested.

Matteo chuckled and said, "It sounds like a movie: Death and Gratitude in Alergia."

"Yes, my friend," I replied, "but mostly gratitude."

# Chapter 13
# Mom and Dad and Antalya

At the beginning of these stories, I recounted that seventeen years ago, my parents were killed on Highway 1 in California. It was a day I still avoided dwelling on and a period I tried to forget. Though their deaths prompted me to change the direction of my life, I don't see it as somehow something good coming from something terrible. The tragedy still haunts me.

At the beginning of these stories, I recounted that seventeen years ago, my parents were killed on Highway 1 in California. It was a day I still avoided dwelling on and a period I tried to forget. Though their deaths prompted me to change the direction of my life, I don't see it as somehow something good coming from something terrible. The tragedy still haunts me.

Their funeral was a blur. I recall being in a daze as I organized and attended the services before returning to school and sitting in classes feeling numb.

When I'm out sailing, I focus on the present moment. I try to squeeze out everything that life has to offer every day without dwelling on the past.

When some of my parent's friends, who are now living in Antalya, Turkey, invited me to visit them, I was hesitant. After all these years, why were they reaching out to me now? Did I really want to be reminded of my parents and have to go over those painful memories? Did I want to know someone who knew my mom and dad?

It took me a while, but eventually, I decided to accept Carolyn and Jonathan's invitation.

Apart from my parents' friends, Antalya has always fascinated me; it is a beautiful place I have wanted to visit for years. Known as the Turkish Riviera, the area has crystal-clear waters, stunning beaches, and mountains near the sea. Since Antalya draws a lot of expats, and they can be a mixed bag, I planned to head directly to Kas, a nearby beach town that is more lowkey and less touristy. I wanted to swim and relax for a few days before meeting Carolyn and Jonathan in Antalya.

How can I describe Kas? It's like the bohemian little brother of the famous Antalya. Its turquoise beaches, relaxed vibe, and live evening music were the perfect introduction to this part of Turkey. I spent four days canoeing over the sunken city at Kalekoy, exploring the ancient amphitheater at Antiphellos, and hanging out on the beaches where I swam, drank, ate, and met some British expats. I was completely relaxed when I set off for Antalya.

Carolyn and Jonathan were like mysterious figures from another life. I recall they had three younger boys who always wanted to play soccer whenever we visited their house. I also remember having barbecues, going on boating trips, and spending some holidays together. However, they were my parents' friends, and due to the age difference, I didn't develop a close bond with their kids.

But I've discovered that sometimes the most fulfilling experiences in life come unexpectedly rather than from planning. So, I set sail from Kas to Antalya with an open mind, eager to see what the universe had in store for me.

After securing my boat at the marina, I sent a message to Carolyn saying, "I'm here!". It didn't take long for them to respond as I heard a woman calling out to me just five minutes later. "Jovanny, is that you?" I climbed onto the deck to find a trim and fit-looking older couple wearing colorful shirts, shorts, straw hats, and sandals. "Carolyn, is that you? And Jonathan?" I hopped from my boat and hugged them both.

"Is this boat yours?" Jonathan asked. I nodded and offered them a tour. "The tour will take one minute, tops," I said as I led them below to see the kitchen, sleeping, and living area. "Does it have a motor?" he asked. "Yes, but I try to use it only in emergencies or when there is no wind." Jonathan nodded. It was obvious that he was interested in boats. "Do you want to go out along the coast tomorrow for a sail?" I asked. He glanced at his wife before answering. "That would be wonderful! Carolyn, what do you think?" She smiled. "I think Jovanny is here to relax, so if that works for him, fine."

Jonathan added, "It doesn't have to be tomorrow, Jovanny. You've been sailing a long way; relax, and we can go out in a few days. Now," he began, changing the subject, "Where are your things?" I looked at him, not understanding. Carolyn broke in, "You're staying with us, Jovanny. The boys have all grown and moved out. More on that later. But we have plenty of rooms." I looked around at my things scattered everywhere. "Why don't I stay here tonight? I can organize my stuff and then come and stay with you tomorrow." They both nodded as we climbed back up onto the pier.

We headed towards the town center, and after a few minutes, we arrived at Hadrian's gate. Jonathan shared some history as we stood beneath one of the triple arches. "Emperor Hadrian visited here in 130 AD," he said. He then pointed upwards and invited me to look up. Above us, we could see floral motifs and rosettes carved from the white stone.

Jonathan continued, "These designs represent life. The Romans wanted to express how the empire's life passed through the imperial leader and emanated throughout the empire, even here in

Antalya. The floral designs honor Emperor Hadrian because they signify the life of the empire that flowed through him when he visited this spot two thousand years ago."

Jonathan's enthusiasm for history was infectious. "I love to touch the stone," Carolyn chimed in. "It makes me think about the people who walked under these arches in the past. I wonder what they felt when they brushed this wall, rushing into or out of the city, chatting with friends, going to the market or temple. Somehow, touching it connects me to history." I, too, touched the stone, then reached down and ran my hand over the grooves worn away in the street stones by ancient chariots and carts coming in and out.

We continued through the old town. "The historical center is called the Kaleici; since our house is on the outer edge, we get to walk through these beautiful winding streets to get there. It still has the flavor of an ancient city, even though there are many tourists," Jonathan said.

As we turned down a pedestrian street, Carolyn added, "There are almost 150,000 expats living in Antalya now; many Brits, Americans, and Russians... from all over. We rode that expat wave sixteen years ago before the housing prices skyrocketed." "But why did you leave California to live here? What inspired you to do that?" I asked. "Tomorrow," she replied. "Tomorrow, we can step into the past. Today, let's stay in the present." Jonathan agreed, then continued, "Now, Jovanny, I want to show you an amazing view. We are heading to the Keçili Park viewing area; trust me, it is worth it."

We soon found ourselves standing on a glass platform hanging from the cliff. The flimsy platform seemed to suspend us inside a magnificent view of the sea, the mountains, the marina, and the Mermerli beach. "There's your boat!" Carolyn called out while pointing at the marina.

Jonathan smiled and made the past come alive again. "You can see the layers of history from up here. What started as a village in the 4th century BC evolved into an important town under King Bergama, a powerful king in the 2nd century BC. He built the fortification walls and improved the harbor. Things exploded when Antalya became the crossroads for trade with the eastern Mediterranean. Then, of course, the Romans took over the entire area and put their stamp on it with new roads, buildings, and monuments. Now, if you look over there," he said, pointing in another direction, "you see Broken Minaret; that was a Byzantine church before being converted into a mosque. This area was completely Christian and under the rule of Byzantium. But in the 11th century, the Seljuks invaded and turned the churches into mosques, giving the city the Ottoman flavor it has today. Is that enough history for you, Jovanny?" he chuckled. "No, no, it's interesting," I responded. "The more I learn about an area, the more interesting it becomes."

"Shall we?" Carolyn said, taking my arm and continuing to walk.

# Onward

We dodged tourists, tables, and vendors while strolling along the ancient streets. Although the Ottoman architecture was beautiful, the area had become a tourist trap. Carolyn must have sensed my discomfort as she suggested we take a different route. "Don't worry," she reassured me, "we don't live in the historical center. Our home is about ten minutes away from the tourist zone." Her words put me at ease.

We soon found ourselves on a tiny street without any tourists or shops. "Wow!" I exclaimed, finally able to appreciate the beauty without any distractions. "We know the scenic route," Jonathan said as we turned another corner onto a quiet street lined with flowers and historical houses. "This is what Antalya was like when we first moved here!" he exclaimed, his arms outstretched. "Before tourists and expats like us discovered it, Antalya was peaceful, charming, and beautiful. But now, most of these buildings are rentals, and residents have moved to the outskirts like us."

As we strolled past other well-maintained historic houses on the tree-lined streets, I asked Carolyn about her children. "If you remember, we have three boys," she began. "The eldest, John Junior, works in the engineering field in Athens. Our second son, Charles, lives in London with his husband. And the youngest, Omar, who you may not remember because he was small when we left California, is studying architecture in Milan. So they have all flown the nest, and here we are, just the two of us in this big house."

"Do they come to visit?" I asked.

"Yes, or we visit them. We see each other two or three times a year, at least. However, Charles hasn't been here in a while..." she trailed off.

"Is that because...?" I began.

She gave me a knowing look. "Don't get me wrong," she said, "Antalya is a great place to live and raise a family. But Turkish culture is somewhat homophobic, which doesn't work for Charles. He prefers for us to visit him or to meet in another place. He is tired of having to be 'careful,' and we understand that."

We walked away from the historical center and strolled down a residential street for a few blocks until Jonathan exclaimed, "We're home!" We halted in front of a two-story yellow stucco villa with stone accents. The property had a large yard with a lawn and an inviting porch with a table and chairs set out. "Wow! Suburban living in Turkey; I love it!" I exclaimed. Carolyn chuckled and added, "There's a pool in the backyard that we put in for the boys. We know, typical Americans. There's even a built-in barbeque in the backyard. The only thing missing is a swing set and an American flag!"

The house's interior looked modern, light-filled, lived-in, and comfortable. "If you want to stay here, here is your bedroom and bathroom," Jonathan said, opening a door. They were so gracious; "Yes, I will come to stay with you tomorrow," I promised again. Carolyn clapped her hands.

"How about a drink?" Jonathan asked. Before I replied, Carolyn asked if we wanted to go to the terrace. "We were planning to grill up there tonight if that works for you," she said. I gave them a thumbs up.

We took the stairs that led to their rooftop terrace, where they had arranged a beautiful table with elegant dishes, glassware, candles, and outdoor lights around the perimeter. "We have an outdoor kitchen here," she said as she brought over a few bottles of chilled wine and Turkish beer. I gestured towards the beer, and Jonathan took out two chilled glasses, poured, and sat down next to me, inviting Carolyn to join us. "I will start the steaks in a minute," he said, reading her mind.

Carolyn sipped her wine while Jonathan and I quickly finished our ice-cold beers before she had finished half her glass. "Sorry, thirsty," I said as Jonathan grabbed two more. "Jovanny, we are so happy you accepted our invitation to come," he said, handing me a bottle. I nodded, but I was still perplexed by the invitation. So when Carolyn asked if I had any questions about life in Antalya, I blurted out, "Why now? I'm happy you contacted me, don't get me wrong. It means a lot to me to reconnect with you. But what prompted you to reach out now, after sixteen years? It must have taken some time to track me down." As soon as I finished speaking, I regretted asking the question because it sounded rude.

Carolyn and Jonathan looked at each other as if asking, "Should you tell him, or should I?" Then Jonathan nodded, and Carolyn began. "I'm leaving for London in a few weeks to stay with Charles," she said. "But the real reason for the trip is my diagnosis. I have a fairly aggressive form of cancer that we need to beat; once I start treatment...well, it will be a long road. Before starting, we wanted to see you," she said. Carolyn paused a moment, took a breath, and then continued. "Looking at one's mortality without flinching is hard, but it also makes you think about your life, choices, and how you got here. Though I promised not to go into the past until tomorrow, I will say this one thing. Your mom was my best friend, and it shook me to the core when your parents passed away. We always wanted to live abroad, and when they were gone, it was time. We left, started a new life here, and never looked back. But, this last year, I began to reflect on my life, especially after I was diagnosed.

"We have a wonderful life here, but sometimes I regret disappearing from California and losing touch with you and our other friends," Carolyn said. "Jonathan knows me well, and when I finally confided in him, he suggested we track you down and invite you to visit. That's how we ended up here." Her eyes filled with tears as she continued, "Welcome, Jovanny. Welcome, welcome, welcome." She reached across the table and clinked her wine glass against my beer.

# Onward

Jonathan reached over and squeezed his wife's hand. Then he rose and got busy cooking steaks while Carolyn continued talking. "Tomorrow, if you would like, we can take you to an amazing place." "I'm always up for something amazing," I replied. "Have you heard of the ancient theater in Aspendos?" she asked. I always tried to research before visiting a place, so I knew a little about it. "Isn't it said to be the best-preserved Roman theater in the world?" I responded. She smiled. "Yes, and it's only about half an hour away. You'll have an unforgettable experience of the past there."

Her words proved to be prophetic.

After dinner, they guided me through the winding streets at night back to the marina, which I wouldn't have found alone. I had a peaceful night's sleep and met them in the morning. We drove from Antalya to Aspendos, which took less than an hour but seemed like a completely different world.

Leaving the hustle and bustle of Antalya and driving through the fields where the city of Aspendos once stood was like being on a crowded beach one minute and finding oneself on an empty sea the next. The area seemed so deserted until I saw the theater rising from the landscape and towering over its surroundings like a cathedral floating above a lost world.

"The Romans built this theater around 150 AD during the reign of Marcus Aurelius," Jonathan explained. "But the city dates back to at least the fifth century BC. Jovanny, you are about to enter the best-preserved theater of the ancient world!" He clapped me on the back in excitement. "Do you want to take some photos here outside?" Carolyn asked before we entered. I shook my head. "I stopped taking selfies years ago. I prefer to experience it instead of trying to hold onto it."

We walked through the entrance and onto the stage of the vast arena that could seat 10,000 spectators. The intricate stone wall backdrop behind us was breathtaking. I turned in a circle and exclaimed, "Wow!" The past seemed to rush upon me as the voices of ancient actors and spectators blended with those of tourists milling around. I walked over to the stone wall and put my hand on one of the carvings, imagining who touched that spot when the Roman Empire was still robust. The thoughts and images of that era seemed to travel from the stone, through my arm, and into my mind. Suddenly, I heard Carolyn's voice, "Jovanny, Jovanny, are you alright?" I shook my daze off and replied, "Yes. Truly amazing." She smiled.

"We can experience the incredible acoustics if you climb to the top. You two go up there to see if you can hear me speak," Jonathan suggested.

We started climbing the many stairs, and Carolyn was huffing and puffing. I offered my arm, and we soon reached the highest level. We found a shady spot to sit and signaled Jonathan that we were ready. At first, he spoke in a low voice, and we could only see his mouth move. He tried again at a higher volume, and we could finally make out his words. I gave him a thumbs-up.

Then he waved at us, signaled for us to watch, and took a paper from his pocket. Looking across the theater at its imaginary spectators, he began reading a paragraph from Shakespeare's "As You Like It," using his arms for dramatic effect.

*All the world's a stage,*
*And all the men and women merely players;*
*They have their exits and their entrances,*
*And one man in his time plays many parts,*
*His acts being seven ages.*

*At first the infant,*
*Mewling and puking in the nurse's arms.*

*Then, the whining school-boy with his satchel*
*And shining morning face, creeping like snail*
*Unwillingly to school.*

*And then the lover,*
*Sighing like furnace, with a woeful ballad*
*Made to his mistress' eyebrow.*

*Then, a soldier,*
*Full of strange oaths, and bearded like the pard,*
*Jealous in honour, sudden, and quick in quarrel,*
*Seeking the bubble reputation*

# A Life on a Sailboat

*Even in the cannon's mouth.*

*And then, the justice,*
*In fair round belly, with a good capon lined,*
*With eyes severe, and beard of formal cut,*
*Full of wise saws, and modern instances,*
*And so he plays his part.*

*The sixth age shifts*
*Into the lean and slippered pantaloon,*
*With spectacles on nose and pouch on side,*
*His youthful hose, well saved, a world too wide*
*For his shrunk shank, and his big manly voice,*
*Turning again toward childish treble, pipes*
*And whistles in his sound.*

*Last scene of all,*
*That ends this strange eventful history,*
*Is second childishness and mere oblivion,*
*Sans teeth, sans eyes, sans taste, sans everything.*
(As You Like It, Act 2 Scene 7)

Jonathan finished his performance, and Carolyn and I clapped and cheered. He bowed and waved goodbye as he exited from the right stage. We sat in the shade and enjoyed the soft breeze while looking down at the crowds.

Carolyn said, "Sometimes I feel like my life is a play. I enter and play different roles. Friend, partner, wife, adventurer, and then I exit. Sometimes, I enter again later, and we continue the drama. We all have our lines, actions, and movements, and we weave a story with our words and actions, creating something we call 'life.'" She looked wistful.

Feeling a sense of intimacy with her, I asked her something that had been on my mind. "Carolyn, can I ask what type of cancer you have?" She took a deep breath. "Breast cancer. It has metastasized. Before you ask, I think I will be fine. They tell me that my chances of survival are at least fifty percent. But the road ahead will be long."

"I am sorry," I said.

"I am too, Jovanny, but I am also hopeful. Life has been too full to end at this point."

Carolyn and I were sitting on the upper level while tourists milled around the stage below. The sun was quite bright, and a gentle breeze was blowing.

There was a comfortable silence between us until Carolyn asked, "Do you ever think about your parents?" I paused for a moment and answered her honestly, "Rarely." She looked surprised, and I continued explaining. "I first avoided thinking about them because the sorrow was too great. I just wanted to leave the entire tragic thing behind, like a scene in a play that's over. The agony of wondering how it happened, the memory of the police officer banging on my door, the drive to Big Sur to the scene of the accident while hoping it was a mistake, then making funeral arrangements...it was all too much. So, I decided to leave it all behind. When I did think of them afterward, I turned my mind away. I guess I just got used to that."

Carolyn nodded. "Your mom and I were close. Would you mind if I talked with you a bit about her?" I nodded; I was ready to face that part of my past.

"I know where you got your adventurous spirit from; it was her. Your dad was the planner; he had to be since he was trying to run and build his business, send his son through college, and make a good life for his family. Your mom and I were of a different type. Do you know that your parents planned on eventually doing what we did? Someday, they planned on moving from California to become expats. They hadn't decided where yet; we hadn't either, for that matter. But she planned to help you complete college, start your career, and then move abroad. At first, your dad resisted, but he softened and eventually told your mom he wanted to be part of her dream. We even talked about doing that together, your parents and us!"

I was looking at Carolyn wide-eyed. "No, I didn't know any of that," I said.

"Your mom had a gypsy spirit, like me," she continued. "That's why we got along so well.

"But," I began, "why didn't they talk about this with me?"

Carolyn paused to reflect and then turned to me. "I think she didn't want you to think that you were holding them back. As far as I know, she didn't discuss the idea with anyone besides Jonathan and me."

"Wow, 'Mom, the adventurer,' the traveling nomad! I never thought of her like that," I said.

Looking at the stage area below, I could imagine my mom walking out, taking a bow, laughing, and rejoicing in life.

I then asked Carolyn to tell me about my dad.

Carolyn laughed. "Your dad was a super responsible person compared to your mom, who was more of a dreamer. It was exactly like Jonathan and me; we balance each other, and I think that was the same for your parents. Your dad was very practical and had to be able to start a successful boating business. He was amazing because he didn't want a 9-5 job or end up in some office. He loved the water, so he decided to figure out how to build a career around that love. Maybe you already know this, but he started by cleaning boats at the pier, and that's how he eventually gained the trust of boat owners, who gave him more responsibilities. Your dad was great with his hands and could fix just about anything. He saw the need for a boat repair service in the pier area, which evolved into his own boat repair and sales business. Your dad didn't take life passively; he also had a dream and made it a reality. Maybe that's why it was harder for him to dump it all and teach English in some foreign country." Carolyn laughed and added, "I don't blame him! Our decision to come here seems crazy when I think about it now."

Carolyn was bringing me back into my parents' world, a world I knew little about and had avoided for years.

"How did you end up here?" I asked.

"I've learned," Carolyn said, "that it is often the most painful circumstances that reveal what is most important in life." She seemed to grow emotional. "When your parents passed..." she cleared her throat and continued. "When they passed, it was like a part of me was gone. I was left stunned for a long time and fell into a deep depression. However, I knew that I had to be strong for our three boys and not let my loss affect them. So, for a while, I pretended to be fine, and I must admit, I think I did a good job. But Jonathan saw right through me and knew that my happiness was just a façade and that the peace of mind I pretended to have was fake.

"So, about six months after your parent's funeral, Jonathan sat me down and asked what it would take for us to become....well, if not happy, at least content again. I was thinking about our jobs, kids, family, friends, money, house, bills, and mortgage - everything we deal with daily. But when I thought about it, I couldn't find happiness in any of those things. Does happiness come from having a great job, being financially secure, living near our relatives, or just being there for our boys at all their school events and sports games? None of it felt right, so I told Jonathan, "I don't know." I feel bad for him now when I look back because that was a really tough time for us."

# Onward

Carolyn took a deep breath, looking down at the ancient stage below. "Then something extraordinary happened. A few weeks after that unresolved conversation, some friends of ours returned from traveling around the Mediterranean. They visited various countries, including Turkey, and described life in each place. They showed us photos and home movies they had taken along the way, and one of those photos was taken here, inside this theater! When I saw it, I was in awe. I remember telling my husband, 'I want to go there!' He was probably relieved that I was finally interested in something. To make a long story short, we came here on vacation with the boys a few months later. By chance, we met several expats who told us about the new life they had established here, free of the rat race they left behind in the US and UK. Their stories renewed our old dream of living in another country, and I remember feeling happy for the first time in ages. Then, something bizarre happened during the last few days of our visit. We met a couple from the US who had been living here for about ten years. They had decided to move back to the States because of their grandchildren. They had been working as English teachers at one of the local schools and asked if we would be interested in taking their positions. It seemed ridiculous, but that afternoon in our hotel room, I turned to Jonathan and said I wanted to move here. He didn't skip a beat and replied, "So do I." That was less than a year after your parents passed, so it's almost seventeen years now."

The theater was now bustling, with tourists going up and down the stairs. As I reflected on what she had just said, she asked, "Is that too much of an information dump?" I laughed and said, "Not at all. I am just taking it all in."

It was strange to think there were so many parts of my parent's lives that I knew nothing about. They were just my mom and dad, not fully formed individuals with their own interests and aspirations. I couldn't help but wonder if they would be living in Antalya today, just down the street from Jonathan and Carolyn, had they not died.

I was trying to wrap my mind around Carolyn's story and what it revealed.

After a few minutes of silence, I asked Carolyn, "Do you still think of them?" She nodded. "I think of your parents, especially your mom, every day, but it wasn't always like that."

She paused and took a deep breath. "When we first moved here, everything was so new that it was easy to be in the present and not cling to the past. But after we felt settled here - which took a long time - I discovered that I could remember your folks without the pain that I had before. My perspective began to change, and I realized how lucky I was to have friends like your mom and dad. Little by little, a sense of gratitude started to creep into that space occupied by loss. I haven't had a friendship again like that, but I am now so grateful that I knew your parents. And now, meeting you again, it's as if I see your mom again, living her dreams, but this time through you."

We got up and walked towards the stage area to look for Jonathan. About halfway down, Carolyn asked, "Do you ever miss her?"

"I tell myself I put all that behind me also," I said. "But yes, I miss them."

We continued in silence.

We walked across the stage and into the vast archeological area behind it. In the distance, we saw Jonathan exploring the other ruins scattered across the countryside. All around us were the remains of a Roman aqueduct, an acropolis, and other partial walls. Although these were less well preserved than the theater, they echoed the past.

Jonathan motioned us to the aqueduct and excitedly said, "Jovanny, put your hand on this and feel the Roman craftsmanship!" I reached over and touched the bricks while looking at the theater in the distance, the remains of the ancient city scattered around us, and Carolyn and Jonathan standing in front of me, smiling. Somehow, I felt my parents there, too, standing with us, looking out, smiling, happy, and content to be in that place with those they loved.

Suddenly, Jonathan put his hand on his stomach as it growled. "No snacks, honey. We didn't think about that," Carolyn said. "Maybe we should head back to grab lunch," she suggested. Without a word, Jonathan turned and headed towards the car. "He gets grumpy when he's hungry," she laughed.

After leaving the ancient world, we arrived back in modern-day Antalya in less than an hour.

We went to a nearby cafe for lunch and had a simple yet incredible meal. Afterwards, I felt tired and wanted to take a nap. Carolyn kindly suggested that we meet for dinner and that she could cook at her house. She even offered to let me stay over if I wanted to. However, I felt like spending time alone, so I declined and told them I would relax on my boat for the rest of the day and evening. I promised to bring my things in the morning. Carolyn seemed to understand immediately. She leaned over, kissed me on the cheek, and repeated, "We are so happy you came, Jovanny."

As I lay on my bed that afternoon, thoughts of Carolyn's words and my parents' memories swirled around my head. Eventually, I fell asleep and dreamt about my mom. In the dream, she wasn't dead. We just thought she had died, but she and my dad had survived and had amnesia, and nobody knew who they were. I discovered they were still alive; when I found them, their amnesia disappeared, and we were all together again.

Then I woke up.

I wasn't feeling up to going out, so I decided to make dinner in my boat. I brought a bowl of spaghetti upstairs and sat on the deck as the sun set.

# Onward

I watched as the clouds turned from yellow to orange with streaks of red. My mother had always loved sunsets.

Then something happened that had never happened before.

I wept for mom and dad.

Somehow, it felt OK to cry.

I realized I had choices in dealing with their loss. I could walk around it, through it, or sit in the middle of it.

I've always chosen to walk around their passing, as not thinking about it seemed easier. Being depressed, or staying in the middle of it, appeared to be the only alternative. But now I saw another way; walking through it meant I could mourn their loss and feel sadness without getting stuck.

I longed for the gratitude that Carolyn spoke of; I wanted to think of my parents and be thankful, but the only way to get there was to travel through the churning waters of grief before getting to the tranquil sea. It was time.

Tears ran down my cheeks as the first stars appeared. At one point, I got choked up and caught myself saying out loud, 'Mom…'. I looked around to make sure nobody heard.

I eventually went to bed but slept very little due to intense emotions. At around 3 a.m., I got up and went to the deck. I was amazed by the sight of the stars in the Milky Way shining so brightly that I could almost touch them.

Looking at the universe, I suddenly felt a strong feeling of belonging. It might sound crazy, but I felt an inner voice telling me I was loved. I was surprised and said out loud, "What the fuck?"

The voice repeated, "You are loved, Jovanny."

I felt a wave of peace and comforting love come over me.

"Thanks, mom. I love you and dad, too," I said, tears in my eyes.

I eventually went back to bed and slept like a log.

When I woke up, I felt a sense of peace and gratitude that I hadn't experienced in decades.

As I made my morning coffee, I chuckled and said, "Wow, you were amazing parents. Thank you."

Since that day, I remember my mom and dad with gratitude.

I thank Carolyn, Jonathan, and Antalya for that gift.

We saw many other sights, took a boat trip to the falls, met other expats, and had incredible times at the beautiful beaches.

However, my most precious memory of Antalya is visiting the theater at Aspendos, where the past and present embraced.

# Chapter 14
# God in the South of France

I've been sailing to the south of France for many years. The beautiful port in Nice, the stunning architecture, the charming surrounding towns, the breathtaking landscapes, and the lovely women always draw me in. But beyond all that, there's something about the south of France that I just can't put my finger on. There's a softness to the light that's just different from anywhere I've ever been. Only those who've been there can really understand what I'm talking about.

I met Pierre and his wife, Lili, on one of my first trips.

After colliding with rocks during rough waters, I arrived at the port of Nice with a damaged hull. I asked around at the marina, and everyone recommended Pierre as the go-to guy for the job. However, before spending a lot of money, I wanted to ensure that Pierre was the right man for the job. The vague comments provided by people like "Pierre is great," "Pierre can fix anything," and "Pierre is your man" just wasn't enough. I asked around and discovered that Pierre was not trained in boatbuilding, design, or engineering but was a handyman who worked on everything from kitchen cabinets to yacht hulls. Despite my reservations about hiring a jack of all trades, I arranged a meeting with him to discuss the work.

I got directions to his workshop, where I was greeted by a short, stout man a few years older than me. He had short black hair, a mustache, dark eyes, and huge hands. When we shook hands, his crushed mine. "I think you just broke my fingers," I said dryly. It took him a second to see that I was joking.

Upon entering Pierre's garage, I was impressed with the projects he was working on, including rewiring an antique lamp, mapping out a plumbing job, and creating furniture out of a pile of wood. Pierre struck me as someone who was overflowing with natural creative intelligence. He may not have been able to quote Voltaire, but he had the talent to fix any engine, build any house, or solve any electrical or plumbing problem. After showing me some of his projects, Pierre gave me the contact information of some of his clients.

We spent the entire afternoon together, sitting at a table in front of his garage/shop. During our conversation, Pierre asked me about myself and what brought me to the south of France. I shared a little about my life and what drew me to the area.

After a while, Pierre excused himself and returned with his wife, Lili. "Why don't you come to dine with us this evening?" Lili asked. "Excellent cook," Pierre said, winking at Lili and squeezing her hand.

That evening, we had a wonderful dinner, and a deep bond was formed between Pierre and me. Since then, I have visited him in the south of France many times, and we have become close friends. Additionally, Pierre has been my go-to person for any issues with my boat, such as the sail constantly coming loose, the onboard engine making strange noises, or issues with the plumbing below deck. He has been able to diagnose most problems over the phone.

Pierre and Lili are two contrasting individuals. Pierre is a strong man with a big heart, while Lili gives a sense of sophistication when she walks into a room. Lili's tall, slender, and model-like appearance makes a striking impression. Although Lili seems more reflective and reserved than Pierre, they complement each other well and have a relationship that others long for.

Our friendship kept growing until one summer when I returned to Nice, I noticed that Pierre had changed. I called him from the marina to meet up, but he didn't seem like the same person I knew. I said, "My friend Pierre, this is Gio! I just arrived and would love to see you today. Are you at home?" After a pause, he responded with a simple "Yes." I then asked him if he was free to meet up now or later, and after another pause, he replied, "Later." I was perplexed by his brief responses and felt like something was off. I said, "Alright. I will come at eight," but he only replied, "Later," before hanging up.

I rang for Pierre that evening with an uneasy feeling. He is probably just sick with a cold, I told myself. "Yes," he said over the intercom, buzzing me in.

Pierre always had a positive spirit and a smile, but when he opened the door, I saw a man with hollow eyes and a drawn expressionless face. It seemed to take him a minute to realize who I was, and he stepped forward mechanically to give me a double kiss on the cheeks and welcomed me inside.

The house was messy, with dishes in the sink, clothing scattered, and dust everywhere. I blurted out the first thing that came into my head: "Where is Lili?"

With a despondent expression, Pierre slumped into a chair and muttered, "She left me," while looking at the grimy floor.

A few situations in my life have left me speechless, and this was one of them.

Pierre and Lili seemed the perfect couple, a love story I had often boasted about to my other friends. How could she leave him?

I was just as confused as Pierre. "But that doesn't make any sense," I said. Pierre nodded and looked up at me with teary eyes. "No, it doesn't. She didn't tell me everything, but I discovered she had met someone else. This man offered her a better life, different from our working-class one." I still couldn't believe it. "But didn't you notice any signs that she was unhappy or something was wrong?" Pierre looked away, trying to hold back more tears. "I work all the time, even on weekends. So, yes, there were signs, but I didn't see them. She probably got tired of being alone while I was always working, and then she met someone who didn't have to work. This was six months ago, and I haven't heard from her since. I don't even know if she's still in France. I don't think I'll ever hear from her again. How is this possible, Gio?" he asked me, his voice trembling.

He then began to cry.

I had no answers.

I had planned to stay for only a few days, but I realized I needed to extend my stay by a few weeks.

Although he was initially hesitant, I persuaded Pierre to let me hire a house cleaner for the following day. I promised to pick him up at nine and spend the entire day with him. "Can you take the day off tomorrow?" I asked. 'I'm free. No work this week,' he responded. This seemed strange since Pierre was always swamped with work.

Later that day, we went for a stroll in Nice and ended up at a lesser-known beach near the port called La Reserve. We found a cafe overlooking the water where we enjoyed a delicious meal. I ordered grilled fish, sliced fresh tomatoes, a rice salad, and crusty bread. Pierre had a salad nicoise made with tomatoes, green beans, and tuna. We topped off our meal with some white wine mixed with sparkling water. Pierre was quiet during our meal, but I was glad to see him eat. "Would you like to take a walk?" I asked. "Tonight, we can do that tonight," he said.

I returned to my boat for a nap, and we planned to meet for dinner at eight.

Hours later, we met in the town center and walked through Nice's lively and festive streets, but Pierre seemed withdrawn. During dinner, I tried to keep the conversation going, avoiding any topic related to Lili, but Pierre remained quiet and answered only one or two words to my questions about work, day, plans, and life. So, I recounted some of my recent adventures, which he politely listened to, but his mind was elsewhere.

After dinner, we took a short stroll because Pierre wanted to go to bed early.

He was an early riser but was still in bed at nine when I arrived the following morning. My friend was deeply depressed. After he showered and dressed, we headed to our favorite breakfast place near the marina.

After Pierre and I had our coffee, he finally cheered up and even laughed at some of my half-assed jokes. We spent the morning checking out our favorite spots in Nice. However, as the day went on, Pierre seemed to retreat into his own world and stayed that way for the rest of the day. It was a real pain in the butt to spend time with him when he was in that state, but he's my friend, and I've been a pain in the butt too. That afternoon, we again went our separate ways until dinner time.

Before returning to my boat, I asked around about Pierre at the marina. I was told that his work habits had become erratic-showing up late, mixing up his bills, and leaving projects unfinished. I knew I had to help him, but I wasn't sure how to do it. I decided to chat with him about it the next day.

The same thing happened in the morning when we had planned to meet at nine. When I arrived at Pierre's house, he was still sleeping. However, the house was tidy, except for some dirty dishes in the sink.

I wasn't sure what to say as we headed to our breakfast spot. Was it even my place to be concerned about Pierre's emotional state and work habits? Should I say something or just be his friend? Watching his life unravel and not do anything about it was tough. Despite all the inner turmoil, we sat down for breakfast and sipped our coffee. "How are you, my friend?" I asked. Pierre glanced at me, looked at the sea, and said, "Oh, I'm fine. Every day is the same. I'm fine…" He trailed off.

I decided to hold my tongue until we ate. "Do you have any jobs today?" I asked. "A few things. I have a boat at the marina and a plumbing job across town, and I have to return a call from an abbey a few hours away. They need general maintenance, but it's so far away; I'm not sure about that one," he said.

Pierre and I were feeling hungry, so I used my charm to persuade the waitress to prepare an

American-style breakfast consisting of eggs, toast, bacon, and orange juice for me. Pierre, however, opted for a hard-boiled egg, two pastries, and a second coffee.

As we sipped our second coffee after breakfast, I expressed my concern. "I'm a little worried about you, my friend," I said. Pierre interrupted me, "Oh, I am fine." I thought he seemed depressed, so I blurted out, "Well, you seem depressed." Pierre looked at me as if I was crazy. His face stiffened, and he said, "I am not depressed."

I decided not to push the point. Pierre took a deep breath and looked out towards the sea before turning to me and saying, "You know me well, Gio. You know that I am not OK. I don't think I am depressed, but I miss Lili, and I am upset with myself. I know it must have been my fault that she left. I must be as stupid as she thinks I am: a stupid, inconsiderate, selfish man. Worthless. Perhaps she was right in leaving. I miss her, but she was right."

"You're the most generous, caring, hard-working, considerate man I know!" I objected. "This is not your fault; Lili left, not you!" But my words sounded hollow.

"Can we not talk about this?" Pierre asked. "Yes, my friend. I am always here for you." Pierre nodded and continued, "Don't worry about me, Gio. I'm fine. I'm not depressed. Sad, but fine."

I extended my stay by two weeks, and Pierre and I developed a routine during that time. We had breakfast together every morning and engaged in small talk. Sometimes, I accompanied him on his jobs, while other times, I spent the day at the beach when he wanted to be left alone.

When the day of my departure arrived, I was feeling sad because I was leaving Pierre in a difficult state. We met at our usual breakfast cafe, and after our coffee, Pierre mentioned that the abbey had contacted him again about some work. He agreed to take the job on the condition that they provided housing, and they agreed. "I start next week. At least it's stable work for a few months. I've never stayed at a monastery before!" he said, almost laughing.

"That's good, my friend. I will miss you. I will return as soon as I can," I said. As we hugged, Pierre whispered, "I am grateful for you, my friend."

After leaving, I often thought of my friend Pierre. However, due to adverse weather, prior commitments, and logistical issues, it took me a year to return to Nice.

Pierre knew I was arriving but had a message waiting for me at the marina. He was tied up but would wait for me at the abbey. He also left instructions on where to find his car keys, how to get to the abbey, and even where his house keys were if I wanted to stay in Nice before leaving. I was excited to see him again, so I quickly packed my things, jumped into his car, and drove off.

As I was getting closer to the monastery, my GPS went wild. It kept telling me to take a U-turn and then go in the opposite direction after driving for a few miles. After going around in circles for about forty minutes, I got annoyed and called Pierre. However, he didn't answer. So, I sent him a text: "I'm lost. GPS can't find you." A minute later, he replied with a different address: "Try this address instead. It's on 'Way of the Abbey'." I typed it in, and it worked! I got there within fifteen minutes.

I had imagined the abbey as a neglected old building, almost abandoned, sitting in an empty field, surrounded by nothing. But, as I pulled up to the town gates, I found myself in a medieval village with shops, artist studios, and cafes surrounding the monastery. The place was full of cobblestone streets, slate roofs, stone walls, and flowers everywhere. "It looks like Disneyland!" I exclaimed to no one in particular.

Suddenly, I heard a booming voice calling my name, "Gio!!!" It was Pierre, my old friend whom I hadn't seen in ages. I hopped out of the car, and he hugged me and kissed my cheeks. I held him at arm's length and looked at him, "My friend," I said, "you look good. You look really good." I meant every word. There was a light in his eyes and color in his face that I hadn't seen since before Lily left.

Pierre patted my back and grabbed my bag. "Let's get you settled first, and then we can explore," he said. We walked further down the central road, from which I could see side streets with more charming buildings, shops, another outdoor cafe, and trailheads leading up into the wilderness.

"This is not what I expected," I said. Pierre put his hand on my shoulders and opened the door to a building near the monks' house. "This is the guest house where you will stay," he whispered. "It is all taken care of, Gio. Nuns run it; don't worry, they are cool. Meals are included if you let them know beforehand."

One of the nuns suddenly appeared, who seemed to be from India. "Pierre! How are you today?" she asked cheerfully. Rather than answering, Pierre said, "Sister, this is my friend Jovanny. He will be staying with us for three nights, maybe more. Can both of us eat dinner here this evening?" She nodded, smiled at both of us, and gave me my key.

I was about to ask her about payment, passport, and cost. Pierre must have guessed my thoughts as he put his arm across my shoulder, turned me towards the stairs, and gave me a slight push. Then he turned and thanked the sister.

"My friend," he said as I took a few steps up. "I will leave you for a few hours. I'm in the middle of fixing a plumbing problem in the abbey. You can rest or explore. Meet me at the abbey church at 7 o'clock, OK?" I nodded. "I am glad you are here, Gio," he said, looking into my eyes.

Walking up the stairs to my room, I wondered whether a bodysnatcher had taken the Pierre I left last year and replaced him with this duplicate. It looked like Pierre and sounded like him, but the last time I saw him, I couldn't even get two words out of him. Now he says he is glad I am here? What the fuck?

I was restless and curious, so I left to explore the abbey. It consisted of two structures - the monastery where the monks lived and the abbey church. I entered the monastery through an ajar door and found myself in a cloister with a garden, an old stone well, and a partly enclosed corridor with faded frescoes. It was a peaceful little oasis. The glass double doors leading to the area where the monks lived were locked, and there was a sign in French indicating that monastery tours were only available three times a day. Visitors were not allowed outside those times, but I assumed that Pierre would be able to get me in later. I left the monastery and found myself in the medieval village surrounding the abbey.

As I explored, I stumbled upon a back cobblestone alley that twisted and turned behind stone houses and shops. It led me to the piazza in front of the abbey church. I took a moment to appreciate the church's beauty, which was a blend of different architectural styles dating back to the 12th century. I sat down on a stone bench and gazed up at the magnificent facade, which made me feel small in comparison. I heard gentle music coming from inside the church and decided to investigate. However, it was too dark to see anything, and just as I walked in, the monks began their Gregorian chant prayers.

# Onward

I sat at the back of the church to let my eyes adjust to the dim light as I allowed myself to be carried by the soothing Gregorian chant. Though I usually walk a fine line between belief and indifference, in that moment, it was easy to feel the divine presence as I listened to the prayers.

I admired the historical blend of Romanesque and Gothic elements that created a serene and beautiful atmosphere. However, I couldn't help but notice a few modern statues and art pieces that didn't quite match the church's historical flavor. I also saw an unattractive gold, yellow, and orange room to the left of the sanctuary, which turned out to be an attempted modern side chapel that didn't quite fit in.

As my eyes adjusted to the light, I could make out the choir area behind the altar, where about fifteen monks were chanting. I was surprised to see that most of them were younger than me.

Later in the day, Pierre explained that they were a diverse and international community from Sri Lanka, Nigeria, Italy, and France. Once the service ended, the monks filed out, leaving only one behind. He had stayed to sweep the rice off the church floor from an earlier wedding ceremony.

Pierre appeared from a side door and gestured for me to follow him. He was standing next to a young monk dressed in black robe, broom in hand. The monk was in his twenties, had short brown hair, blue eyes, and a relaxed expression. When I approached, Pierre pointed at the monk and said, "Gio, that's a monk!" I looked him up and down, and he did the same; we all laughed. "Baptiste, this is my good friend Gio. Gio, this is Baptiste, the first monk you've ever met!" I extended my hand, and we shook hands while Baptiste said, "I hope I make a good impression. And if not, I hope someone else will make a better one!" He smiled and turned to Pierre. "What are you guys doing later?" Pierre looked at me and replied, "We'll have an aperitif, then dinner at the convent. After that, we can meet you at the cafe for a drink if you can come." Brother Baptiste agreed. "See you then!"

"My friend," Pierre said, turning to me. "I have some work to finish up: leaky pipe. Meet me in half an hour at the cafe on the main street with the outdoor tables. And please order a Spritz for me."

After leaving the church, I strolled through the village and climbed a hill. I found a bench on which I sat and enjoyed the view of the valleys below. Though the hill wasn't very high, the view was serene, with the sun painting the sky a blend of pink, orange, and purple.

I returned to town and passed several antique shops and artist studios before reaching our cafe. Although I'm not much of a liquor drinker, being in this place made me crave vodka and ice while I waited for Pierre.

It was a warm evening, and the vodka over ice was perfect. The cafe had set up eight tables on the cobblestone street, facing shops and a bakery. Several tourists stopped by the bakery, gazed into the windows, and went in and out with their food.

# Onward

I couldn't help but wonder why so many visitors came here. Apart from the abbey, the town didn't seem particularly religious. However, it was incredibly beautiful, like a scene out of a medieval painting. Perhaps it was the beauty that drew the crowds.

"My friend! Where is my Spritz? Did you start without me?" a booming voice interrupted my thoughts. I looked up and saw Pierre approaching our table with a smile. I signaled the proprietor, and we had his drink on the table in no time.

"I can't tell you how glad I am that you are here, Gio!" Pierre said after we toasted our friendship. I looked at his shining eyes and said, "The change in you is amazing. You look so much happier. Are you?" Pierre looked into space, paused, and replied, "I am content, and that is enough. I don't know if happiness is for me, at least in this life." I chuckled and teased him, "Now you're sounding like one of the monks!" Pierre laughed and sipped his Spritz. "What is your daily life like here?" I asked.

"You're going to laugh; I know you, Gio. But I will tell you anyway. I start my day at 7 when the monks chant the morning Mass. Yes, Gio, stop making that face! I begin my day with the service at 7. They have five prayer services a day, and most are very short. They chant their 'divine office,' which is a prayer from the Bible set to music. If I am not dealing with a broken pipe or leaky roof, I join them during those times, too. They conclude their day with their night prayer at 9, and I always make that. So the

285

chanting of the monks frames my day and gives me a routine that I had lost after..." Pierre trailed off.

I wanted to distract him from thinking about Lili, so I asked, "So, does the rhythm of life at the abbey give you peace?" Pierre nodded, and I continued, "I can see it, my friend. You seem so serene now." He agreed and replied, "I am at peace. I don't have a long-term plan, but that's alright. The head monk, the abbot, told me he had enough work for me for four to five days per week. When I asked him how long, he said 'permanently,' if that would work for me. This abbey complex is ancient and has been neglected for so long that there is always either repair work or renovation waiting to be done. There's a lifetime of work here."

Curious, I leaned forward and asked, "So what did you tell him?" Pierre took another sip and crunched on a chip before replying, "I told him I would keep my house in Nice and return there every weekend, but my work is here at the abbey for as long as they need me. He seemed happy." I joked, "Wow, Pierre the monk, who would have imagined?" He replied, "The abbot told me I would make a great monk, but because of my marriage..." Pierre's mind seemed to wander to Lili again, but not for long, as he continued, "I needed a routine, a purpose, and a community, and the abbey has given me all three. Who can say it's not God's hand?" He looked at me, and I shrugged, "Who can say?"

Pierre looked me in the eyes and asked, "And how are you, my friend?" I laughed. "When you ask me that question, Pierre, I have to think before saying, 'I'm fine.' Your question deserves more. Let me see… how am I…" I paused to reflect on the past months, what I have been doing, and how I have felt. I wanted to give an honest response.

"I am good, Pierre. I am learning to balance my desire for adventure with my need for belonging. Just sailing into a port, looking at a few buildings, and then moving on to the next destination doesn't work for me anymore. I'm starting to put people before places and see things changing; somehow, my life feels fuller and has a purpose. You know Matteo, of course, and I'm sure you remember Antonio and Giovanna. When I think about my life, I think about Sadiki and Masika, Samuru and Roberto, Charbel and Noam, Khalil and Yara, Carolyn and Jonathan, and my friend Pierre. There are others I can't remember right now, but I'm discovering that mattering to one another makes life more meaningful."

I paused, looked at Pierre, then continued. "Your smile, the peace of mind emanating from you, gives me joy. Right now, with you, I feel happy, content, and grateful." Pierre smiled.

Dinner time arrived, so we quickly finished our drinks and walked over to the nuns' guesthouse.

The dinner was simple but hit the spot: chicken broth served with fresh bread, steamed vegetables, sliced meats and cheeses, house wine, and a somewhat dry homemade yellow cake for dessert.

Two nuns served the food, wearing odd headgear over their veil, which, Pierre explained, represented the crown of thorns. They seemed happy to have us as guests. We were both famished, so our conversation was brief as we eagerly consumed food and wine.

After finishing our meal, we took a little stroll down the deserted cobblestone street and passed by the cafe we had visited earlier. The proprietor called out to us and offered an after-dinner drink. He said we could have a bitter made by French monks, or if we had enough monks for the day, he could offer us a Limoncello made in Italy.

In unison, we both said, "Limoncello!"

While enjoying our drinks and chatting, Baptiste, dressed in his monk's habit, showed up and sat with us. Pierre ordered him a drink and greeted him warmly. Baptiste seemed high-strung, energetic, and passionate. "How was your day, Jovanny?" I filled him in, and then he asked Pierre about our plans while I was visiting. Baptiste seemed disappointed when Pierre told him we would hang out at the abbey for a few days rather than head to Nice.

After some small talk and another drink, Baptiste suddenly said, "Pierre, I have to talk with you about something!" I started to get up to leave them alone, but Pierre insisted I stay. "No secrets here," Baptiste said and continued, "The abbot is going away next weekend! Let's go out and do something! He will be gone for three or four days; come on, Pierre, let's make a plan! I think Brother Jacques wants to come also." Pierre laughed and agreed.

Confused, I interjected, "When the cat's away, the mice play?" Baptiste nodded and replied, "Not only play; they have a party! Finally, we can breathe!" Pierre nodded as if he understood. "I can't stay out late tonight, my friends," Baptiste said as he finished his Limoncello and stood up. "Will I see you tomorrow morning?" "Yes, until tomorrow," Pierre said. Baptiste hugged us both and disappeared down the road to the abbey.

Once Baptiste left, I asked Pierre what was happening in the monastery. "Do they ask you to bring them to Nice for sex?" Pierre laughed and said, "Gio, your mind always goes to sex! I would never be part of that! No, not at all. Baptiste, Jacques, and the other monks here are young; they are only in their twenties! They want to experience life outside the abbey. So, when the abbot is out of town, we take the opportunity to drive to Nice or another nearby town and do things that young people enjoy, such as having a beer, people-watching, strolling along the beach, or watching a movie. We go out as friends; when we return, we are still friends, not accomplices. It's that simple."

I nodded with some skepticism.

My curiosity was aroused, so I asked Pierre to tell me about the other monks. Pierre replied, "They are just like you and me, but with an added dimension that I can't explain. Some monks here are from underdeveloped countries with little education, and they seem to know less about Christianity than I do. Maybe they are here to seek a better way of life or to reach the West. I heard that one of the monks takes money from the collection to support his struggling family. It seems strange; why doesn't he ask the abbot for help? Everybody knows he takes it. But who am I to judge?"

I was taken aback and asked, "A monk who steals? Isn't that a contradiction?" Pierre replied, "The longer I stay here, the more I realize that I don't know someone's circumstances, so I don't judge them. But Gio, listen to me. Despite their flaws, these monks have something that I am grateful for. They somehow connect me with peace. So, I can accept them for who they are, just like they accept me."

Pierre's new outlook made me happy, even though I didn't fully understand it.

"Gio, tomorrow is Sunday. After the noon service, the abbot invited us to have lunch with the monks. I agreed to it because it doesn't happen often. I hope you are OK with it." It would be a new adventure, so I gave him a thumbs-up. We toasted for the last time, drank, and then went to our rooms.

Since Pierre was busy with something the next morning, I decided to visit the abbey church after having breakfast. When I got there, a service was just about to start. Since I had no other plans, I decided to stay and attend the service. As I sat down, the abbot appeared, and the monks started their morning prayer. Pierre was right about their chanting - it could effortlessly transport you to another world. The service was so good that I stayed for the entire duration.

When I walked out, I had a feeling inside of me that I couldn't put my finger on. It was something like peace, gratitude, and happiness rolled into one.

I still had some free time, so I went hiking in the hills above the abbey to check out the views. I climbed to the top of the bluff and saw a great view of the rolling hills in the distance, but there was a parking lot below that I wanted to avoid. So, I continued following the trail and hiked for another 15 or 20 minutes until the trees opened up, and the trail led me to a ridge overlooking a misty valley. I sat on a rock and enjoyed the view, which reminded me of something out of the Lord of the Rings, minus the hobbits.

I lost track of time and kept hiking until I realized the sun was already above me. "Oh fuck!" I said as I checked my watch. It was past noon. I rushed back down the hill and met Pierre at the abbey. He signaled for me to follow him inside the church where we listened to the monks celebrate their Sunday Mass. Right after the service, Pierre led me up behind the altar to the stalls where the monks started to chant their office prayers. I looked at him, surprised that he hadn't mentioned this was part of the plan. He smiled as if he recognized my discomfort.

Pierre sat far away from me on the other side of the choir stalls. I gave him a dirty look, but the monk from Sri Lanka next to me sensed I was confused and let me share his book. I had no idea how their chants worked, but my anxiety slowly subsided, and I started to follow the singing's flow, which echoed within the ancient church.

The service was short, and the abbot concluded it with a blessing. Pierre caught my eye and motioned for me to follow him again.

We exited and went through a few corridors until we arrived at the monks' refectory. I was surprised that the room was small and intimate, but at least Pierre was there. I wanted to sit next to him, but then I saw him standing at the back of one of the four long tables that formed a square along the walls. Just as I was about to sit down, I noticed that all the monks were standing. I looked over at Pierre, but he was looking down. I looked at Pierre as if to say, "Why did you get me into this situation?"

"Gio, just go with it," I told my stubborn self. As soon as the abbot entered, everyone sat down.

I reached for a slice of bread, but then one of the monks began reading a Bible story. I let the slice drop and looked around, since nobody was eating. Instead, they all had their hands folded on their lap. Feeling self-conscious, I looked down at my plate and tried to listen to the reading. When the reading was concluded, the abbot prayed over the meal. Suddenly, the atmosphere changed, and everyone began to relax, eat, and chat. An older bald monk named Paul asked me where I was from. He seemed friendly, and I liked his British accent, so we started to talk. During our conversation, I shared a bit of my story, and he shared a bit of his.

Then, suddenly, the abbot spoke.

"I'm glad you're dining with us, Jovanny! Is that an Italian name?" I stopped chatting with Paul and replied, "It's spelled with a 'J,' not a 'G.' My grandfather on my father's side is from Mexico, while on my mother's side, I have a mix of Italian and other ancestries. Jovanny with a 'J' is a common name in Mexico." The abbot nodded and continued, "Pierre mentioned you're a sailor. How many countries have you visited, and what kind of adventures have you had?" All the monks' eyes were on me, so I thought about what I could share. Eventually, I recounted a few short stories about storms, close calls, and beautiful destinations, but I left out any references to women or relationships.

As two monks began to serve the meal, conversation slowed as we filled our plates. Several monks were Italian, which explained the food served, including the baked ziti with just enough tomato sauce and cheese to make it moist and delicious. Then, another monk approached our table with a platter of meatballs and roasted rosemary potatoes, followed by a salad with sliced tomatoes. After that came the fruit: apples, pears, and figs. A half-eaten large cake was served for dessert, but it looked like something leftover from a party the day before. I took a tiny slice to be polite. After we all had our coffee, all the monks stood, said their prayers, and we all filed out.

Pierre and I followed the others to a beautiful flower courtyard where the monks gathered after their meals. While there, I conversed with Pascal, a French priest/monk around my age. Pascal had a muscular build, dark hair and beard, and green eyes - he didn't look like what I thought a monk would look like. Before entering the monastery, Pascal had a full life; he worked as a lawyer, was engaged to be married, and had plans to start his own business. However, he began to feel restless, which eventually led him to the monastery. Meanwhile, Baptiste was laughing and joking with Pierre and two others.

I found that these monks were more "normal" than I expected. I thought they would all be people trying to escape something, but instead, I saw men like myself and Pierre, just trying to find a meaningful path.

Pierre yawned and then excused himself. "What do you say if we take a nap, my friend? Can we meet at five o'clock, walk on the trails, eat dinner here, and then head to Nice tomorrow? I changed our plans since I worked the weekend; the abbot told me I don't have to return until Wednesday morning." I almost felt sad leaving the abbey the following day; something about this place was getting to me, but I gave him a thumbs up nonetheless.

My friendship with Pierre had grown, so our companionship did not require constant conversation. Hence, we mostly remained quiet during our afternoon hike through the hills, taking in the surrounding beauty. Occasionally, we exchanged comments like "Look at that view!" and "Are you doing alright?".

"I propose that we head to Nice tomorrow morning around nine," Pierre said as we neared the abbey. "We can rest now and meet for dinner in an hour." I gladly agreed as the slow pace of the monastery town made a second nap necessary.

As I lay in bed and reflected on my experiences, I felt grateful. I thought of Pierre and how it seemed like he was being taken care of. Slowly, I drifted off to sleep, feeling that, in some way, I was being taken care of, too.

When the sun set, I woke up from my nap and realized that dinner was being served. I quickly got ready by splashing water on my face and headed downstairs to find Pierre sitting in the garden. I crept over to him to play a joke but then decided to give him his moment. I kicked some gravel to get his attention. "Gio!" he said, rising. "Let's eat!"

Even though we had already had a big lunch with the monks, I wanted to please our sister cooks, so I ate the chicken broth with rice, sliced ham, spinach, bread, and a crisp apple. I drank some sour house wine and toasted our convent meal with Pierre. "Will you come back with me here on Wednesday?" he asked suddenly. "Are you bored?" he continued. "Yes and no," I said. "Yes, you are bored, and no, you will not return," he said jokingly.

"It's the opposite," I clarified. I was here to spend time with my friend. "Will you go to the night prayer service in the abbey?" I asked. Pierre nodded. "Join me if you want. Then we can grab a drink. I am sure Baptiste will join us," he added.

I sat at the back of the church, letting the chanting carry me. I didn't follow the words on the printed cards in the pews; somehow, the monks' singing echoed inside and transported me. I felt immense peace, and the longer I stayed, the more I understood the change in my friend.

"Two cognacs, please, and the good stuff!" Pierre called out to his proprietor friend at the cafe afterward. Since most tourists had gone, and we had the place to ourselves, we pulled up two chairs at the best outdoor table. "Is Baptiste coming?" I asked. "If I know Baptiste, which I do, he will come." We laughed and clinked glasses.

After my second sip, I asked, "What do you get from that service that keeps you returning every night?" Pierre stared at me, trying to determine whether my question was sincere. "Did you understand the words?" he asked, "Or is your French too rusty?" I hesitated, then admitted, "I wasn't paying attention to the words." Instead of scolding me, Pierre continued to explain.

"The night service is known as Compline, and during the service, there is a section where a quote from Simeon in the New Testament is read. Do you know who Simeon was?" I shook my head. "Simeon was an elderly man who had been waiting his entire life to understand his purpose; finally, it was revealed to him. Did you hear the monks chanting these words?" My friend went on to recite the chant.

"' Lord, now let your servant depart in peace, according to your word; for my eyes have seen your salvation which you have prepared in the presence of all peoples, a light for revelation to the Gentiles, and for glory to your people Israel.'"

As he continued, Pierre seemed to see images from the past dance before him.

"Here is this man, Simeon, telling the bystanders that now he can die. There was no greater thing for him to live for than that infant in his arms. He had longed for the divine, which revealed itself in that baby. He could depart once his eyes saw what he had desired his whole life. What others have longed for, he sees, he holds, he touches. I love that prayer. That is why I go every night."

"It reminds me of you," I said.
"Yes, perhaps it is me," Pierre responded.

I spent several weeks with Pierre, but that night at the abbey was one of the most profound moments I had ever experienced. I felt closer to both Pierre and the divine than ever before.

Perhaps God is in the south of France.

# Chapter 15
# Where From Here?

I hope my many experiences on my sailboat over the last fifteen years will result in some wisdom. "My Life Up To This Point" is what I would call this collection of stories.

Living on a sailboat has taught me lessons about other people. While I initially set out with a curious and adventure-seeking mindset, I discovered that relationships matter most. While the beautiful views, amazing beaches, historical buildings, and unique locales continue to draw me, the people I meet along the way impact me the most.

For me, a place has meaning if I can connect with the people, form relationships, or build friendships. These relationships have enriched my life and expanded my horizons.

Compared to when I first set out, I am much more hesitant to judge another person or culture.

Lesson two of my journey is about romance. My nomadic lifestyle doesn't work for everyone, and I haven't met anyone who would embrace it. Every relationship I've been in has led to a tough decision - either I give up on my lifestyle or choose to stay in the relationship. However, having a wife and family isn't compatible with my choices unless I change course. Since I am unwilling to do that, my romantic involvements may never lead to a committed relationship. I have learned to be at peace with that.

The third lesson is about fulfillment and emptiness. My life on the sea has enabled me to form deep bonds like family, giving me joy and fulfillment. But there are times when I feel an emptiness. Is it a longing for something more? Does part of me want a stable land life, with a job, wife, and kids? Perhaps the sense of fulfillment and longing for something more will always be my companions as long as I stay on this course.

The fourth lesson is to treat myself as my best friend. I've made mistakes, hurt others, and made stupid decisions that I am not proud of. I tend to beat myself up long after the other person has moved on. When I catch myself tearing myself down, I've learned to stop and ask myself: "Gio, what would you say to your best friend in this situation?"

Making mistakes is the path to wisdom, and I've accepted that.

There are many lessons that I have learned, but one of the most important ones became clear to me recently. I realized that I was being held hostage by my past. The loss of my parents had left an emptiness in my life that I either ignored or tried to escape from. The memories of their passing continued to haunt me. However, during my time in Antalya, I discovered that I could confront my past, mourn my parents' loss, rediscover their companionship, and move forward without the pain.

The last lesson I learned was the feeling of being taken care of. Whether it was almost losing my life in the Mediterranean, visiting friends in Jerusalem, or staying with Pierre in the south of France, the feeling of being guided, cared for, and even loved gave me a sense of peace that I didn't have at the beginning of my voyage.

My journey continues, and I am filled with gratitude, a sense of belonging, and a continual feeling of adventure.